In My House

No Failure Allowed!

By

Dr. Laurie Roth

*An inspiring, insightful, caring, and funny
guide to overcome the struggles in life.*

*This book is a refreshing reminder of
the power and worth
we all possess.*

Pair-A- Docs Press

Dr. Laurie Roth Worldwide Productions ™

Published by
Pair-A-Docs Press ™
427 S.W. Madison Suite D # 167
Corvallis, OR 97333

First Published in 1996

Copyright © 1996

Illustrations Copyright © 1996

Illustrations by Dr. Laurie Roth

ISBN 0-9654706-0-1

Cover Design by G. Hanson at B & B Litho, Tigard OR

Cover Photo by Lynn DeBon

Edited by Richard Sanders

Printed in the United States of America

Dedication

This book is dedicated to Tom Romero.
He was a dear long time friend and inspiration to all who knew him.
His spirit and memory live on.

Acknowledgments

The following people have been a great source of personal friendship and support to me during the writing of this book and my journey back from pain.

Neil and Joanne Roth • Eddie Roth • Shelley Hunwick
Bonnie Laing • Connie Dougherty • Rex King
Dave Woodward • Lee Chabre
Dick and Paige St. Nicklaus • Michelle Blood
Ron and Dianna Stevenson and the Stevenson Gallery
Jim and Sue Grandon • Joel • Mary and Lon Jensen
Victoria Johnson • John Hanna • Scott Night
Nancy and Frank Pasco • Judy and Sam Samualson
Kirk and Sue Holmberg • Jim Eagon • Jim Snelling
Jim Nicolaides • Glenn Sweeney • ACES and staff
Koke Kokeguchi • Kioko Koyama • Gloria Doidge
Paul and Pamela Newman • Dave Fackler • Doug Henry
Carl Jochums • Georgia Hanson • Lynn DeBon
Everette and Rosanne Taylor • The Romero family
Greg and Alfred • Michael Baker • Father Frank
Walter Hailey • Leticia Johnson • Jack Phillips
Dennis Carter and Falcon Recording Studios • Robert Young
Richard Sanders • Dave Klugee • Lynn Easton

Dan Jacobson • Mike Cooper

All those who offered various financial help and advice along the way,

Thank you!

There is no way in the short pages of this book that I can thank all those wonderful people that have come out of the woodwork to help along the way.

Your faith and support have made all the difference!

Thanks again!

Table of Contents

Introduction
by

Dick Peterson
(of the Kingsmen)

Imagine if you will a striking, multi-talented woman who holds a Ph.D. in counseling, a black belt in Tae Kwon Do and has had a hit tune on the Billboard top 40 charts. Add to those considerable accomplishments 14 successful years as a counselor and businesswoman.

Those are laudable lifetime achievements for anyone, but for one person to have accomplished them all before her 35th birthday is simply extraordinary. That remarkable young woman is Dr. Laurie Roth, whose book it is my privilege to introduce.

Dr. Roth's book is not just a simple success story. It is a story of a talented person who watched almost every structure of her social and professional life collapse within a period of less than six months. During that brief period, Laurie Roth experienced the collapse of a long-term love relationship. The dance song she had recorded that soared to a spot on the Billboard Top 40 Chart plummeted for lack of promised commercial backing. Business losses quickly created personal financial problems, and Laurie Roth found herself in dire personal and professional economic straits. She was without income or a place to live.

On top of all that, her closest friend and the person she turned to most often for emotional support was forced to return home to New Zealand when her visa expired. Laurie Roth found herself in a world of shattered hopes and dreams.

Is it any wonder that for a brief period, Laurie Roth felt helpless in the face of what seemed overwhelming life events? Of that period she writes: At a time in my life when I had so many accomplishments to my credit, I found myself lost, hurting so painfully that the very core of my identity was almost shattered. I had reached a point in my life where I let outside events threaten to overcome and destroy me. I felt helpless. I didn't want to fight. I simply wanted to run or hide. I wanted to avoid the painful realities confronting me.

But Laurie Roth did not run or hide. Instead she fought the most courageous battle of her life against her most formidable opponent her-

7

self. And she won. She won because of sheer determination. If I had to use one word to characterize Dr. Laurie Roth, it would be grit.

In My House is not just the story of how Laurie Roth overcame some very real external forces and every-bit-as-real internal forces that threatened to destroy her life. It is a vivid description of the emotional, mental and physical tools she used to overcome those negative forces. It is a story, I think, important to us all. For which of us hasn't been trapped by events that looked so bleak there seemed to be no way out? Usually, however, we somehow struggle along and finally muddle through. But those actions we took that allowed us to escape are often not very obvious to us. Because they are not obvious and we don't consciously recognize them, we don't know how to call them up when we need them again. We are often doomed to relive our failures.

Dr. Laurie Roth in "*In My House*" explores the actions she took. She started writing this book to help clarify for herself how she had failed and how she had then overcome those failures. But as she wrote, it occurred to her that she was describing positive life forces that all of us can use to better our lives. If you are looking for a guide to life-enhancing positive actions you can use to better yourself, this book is for you.

This book can change your life. Join Dr. Roth as she helps you explore the forces within you that can change your life forever.

Enjoy!

WELCOME

to

MY HOUSE

Preface
by
Dr. Laurie Roth

I believe with all my heart that we all have within us a unique and powerful force capable of being tapped and transforming our entire way of life. I believe that because I discovered it within myself, and I want to share with you what that powerful force is and how you can tap it. Come with me through the pages of this book, and let's explore together one of the most powerful facets of human existence. The facet that distinguishes us from all other creatures on earth is self-awareness.

Self-awareness-such an ordinary, common-sounding term. Yet it is the very process that has allowed humankind to change the face of this earth in ways no other living creature has been able to. It is the painful process by which I overcame the negative forces in my life that almost destroyed me. It is the joyous process that allowed me to unlock those powerful positive forces within me. I want to show you what a powerful tool self-awareness is, and if you will venture with me through the pages before us, I will show you how self-awareness is the key to self-empowerment.

No matter who you are, where you come from or what you have done, you have within you the resources to take the steps necessary to explore and embrace all of who you can be!

SECTION I

REBUILDING

Chapter 1:

Who Made This Mess?

"I threw open the door and gasped at the mess!

Who could have done this?"

One day not long ago I looked a the mess my life had become and wondered if I could survive it.

The song I had written and recorded, that had soared to a spot on Billboard's Top 40, had plummeted as quickly, for want of the promotional support it had been promised and never received.

On the basis of that success and on the promise of the promotional support that was supposed to sustain it, I committed to personal investments I soon found I could not really afford. I was overwhelmed by debt, fell into personal and corporate bankruptcy, was evicted from my home, lost my furniture and car and had to deal with hundreds of phone calls from hostile investors and creditors.

During this same period a long-term love relationship collapsed. Add to all that the fact that I lost my closest friend and main support system, the person I had always turned to when I needed to talk things out. She was a New Zealander and had been forced to leave the country when her visa expired.

Adversity allows us to take stock of ourselves and discover the stuff of which we are made.

Dr. Roth completes another session of Bunji Therapy

During such painful, embarrassing and humiliating times we are often tempted to withdraw into the oblivion of one form of addiction or another or are challenged to recreate ourselves. These are the kinds of situations that draw so many people to the so-called self-help movement. That movement held a strong attraction for me then. But I recognized it for what it was for me then, an opiate, an addictive oblivion, a way to avoid looking at my own weaknesses. For me, I recognized some of the self-help movement as a way to avoid my own strengths, a way of avoiding real change.

Looking back now into this scene of madness I recall the investor withdrawals of promised funds with a kind of painful wonder at how I could have been so gullible. My 20 year dream of being a successful recording artist and songwriter loomed so painfully near as my single charted on the top 40 only to quickly fall off the charts due to lack of promised funds.

It was all so full of clichés and so predictable it was nauseating—it could have been a formula B movie on the big screen. Naïve, small town girl trusts wrong people, plays with the big boys, bites the success carrot, plays hard, risks hard, looses hard, people scatter, and there she stood—frightened, raw, scared and alone. After my eviction I moved on borrowed money to a friend's house where I had a room in a cobweb filled attic. Another friend loaned me a futon to sleep on because my bed had been repossessed. I was grateful for a built-in shelf to put my clothes on—what clothes I had.

The starkness of the contrast was laughable. A few months before I was getting out of limos, doing interviews with music trades and magazines, making music videos. I was the CEO of an independent label with major distribution, was finishing my Ph. D. and was making my way skillfully through the world of fund raising. I had employees, popularity, a dream—a dream that died a painful, expensive death, one without health insurance or a funeral plan.

Join me on a journey into yourself, and let me help you discover the real you.

The most critical question that now faced me was what else died in that avalanche of disasters? Did I die with my dream? And if I died with the dream was my life nothing but smoke and mirrors all along? An unreal image? A wooden Pinocchio that would never become human?

For over a decade I had been a therapist while pushing hard in the music field. I had tested myself, taken risks and pushed the limits of endurance. After the fallout I had a rare chance to look honestly at myself, survey the wounds, integrate my experience into my real self and begin a new way of interacting with others.

I soon learned that there was far more to me and this house of self than meets the eye. I also learned that we all have amazing reservoirs of energy and strength, even while enduring suffering and pain.

I made a choice!

It is my fond hope that together in the pages of this book we will find the key that will unlock the wonderful resources in your house.

I chose to rebuild the <u>foundation of my life</u> and build a new house on it, one with extra insulation, a security system and more windows—more ways of looking out at the world about me. I made up my mind that this new home would be a place of living, loving and learning.

I want to explore with you what my experience as a therapist and what my journey through life's challenges has taught me. I want us to look together at how pain and failure can be the gateway to unbelievable success and inner peace in your career and personal life.

In this book, *In My House*, we will work together to discover and release the powerful and wonderful *you*, no matter what your circumstances may be.

You may just find that the best things in your life already exist but are locked away in those hidden rooms of the heart you had dared not enter because of insecurity and fear of failure.

If you can embrace what pain has to show you, all the possible richness of your life will open up to you.

CHAPTER 2:
USING ADVERSITY TO INCREASE YOUR AWARENESS

"My shaky fingers opened the attic door and strained to see through the layered dust."

There are times in life when we feel so low that everything appears almost like a haze, a fog, drifting, suspended as if we were in an anti-gravity machine, having no idea where or how to land, wondering if we did land if our feet would support the weight? **What most of us don't know is that during these confusing, often devastating, crossroads times of life we have never been closer to success or to finding ourselves, discovering endless wells of energy and cultivating the courage to be real.**

The crossroads of our life are periods of great growth.

You see, there are dark hallways and rooms in our house that we must wander through alone before we are allowed to find the window shades we can throw open to the treasure of light awaiting us in the world outside, a world full of self-revelation and hints of our future.

Accepting pain and admitting our failures is the price we pay for wisdom.

I've heard it said for years about almost any personal or career endeavor: "We have to pay the price, pay our dues to achieve success or wisdom." Just what does that mean? Pay what and whose price? Is part of this price, pain and lonely visitation to our own failures and fears? I say Yes. Absolutely!

Alone and scared in the dark, small hallways of my own fears, I can hear myself breathe—I notice my unsteady breaths, laboring chest. I step slowly, carefully, aware of every foreign bump, of every piece of furniture that may lie before my unsteady feet. I'm aware that my skin

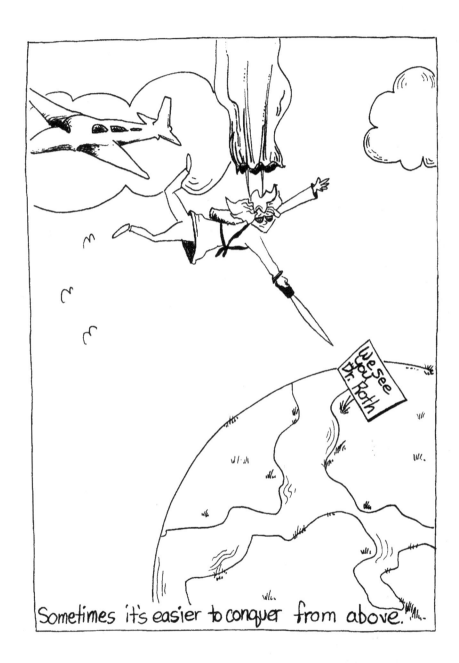

Sometimes it's easier to conquer from above.

crawls with anticipation—anticipation of something yet to be revealed, maybe danger. What I know for sure, though, is that I am painfully *aware*. I feel anxiety, that distant cousin of curiosity masked by fear of the unknown. In that dark passageway of my fear, I feel my heart. Wait a minute...I feel my heart beat! In the dark, lonely and scary place *I feel my heart beat!* I am *present* and am risking and facing the immediate challenge and elementary demands placed in my way *right now*. At this moment I am thoroughly alive and *aware*.

> We are often most thoroughly alive during periods of anxiety and pain.

I am convinced that after years, even decades, of negative conditioning, superficial goal-setting and looking outward to things, events, schedules, opinions and demands, we have almost completely excluded the most powerful and natural healing elements within our house. We have forgotten the primary power source and unique magic of being human—the basic elements of life, elements that adjust to our vision only when we sit in the dim light for some time and allow our surroundings to come into focus. Slowly as we really look, things become clearer and easier to see. The room begins to take shape.

I want to share with you here an experience from my high school days. It taught me something about being fully alive, about caring.

Cindy was the mean machine on campus, on drugs, carried a switchblade and had a black belt—any questions? I was 15 at the time and actively involved in sports, horses and music—definitely not the switchblade type! I couldn't help noticing her in the cafeteria and in my various classes. I could see her body shake from the speed she was on. Most kids avoided her because she was scary looking.

I later found out she had been rejected by her parents and was all but homeless. I really felt bad for her, but how could I make a difference? I felt like such a plain boot scrape with no street smarts. All I knew was that a beautiful person had lost herself and I had to reach out in some way. Even if I was rejected.

So....one day when I found out she was going to another one of her drug parties, I tried to persuade her not to. Of course, I must have had an unrecognized death wish, but oh well! I mustered up my feeble courage and walked up to her in the cafeteria at lunch and told her I cared about her and wanted to encourage her to talk instead of going to her drug party.

She promptly, turned and slugged me right up against the cafeteria wall. I realized the brilliance of my timing as a counselor right then and there. Perhaps someday I'd be a famous counselor in Tea Cup Oregon, population 29 and declining!

After she hit me she ran swearing out of the cafeteria. I ran after her and yelled, "If you go to the drug party, I'll care about you anyway." She of course swore at me and flipped me off. The next day, much to my shock, she approached me and my black eye, gave me a silver cross and letter in which she apologized for hitting me and yelling at me. She explained how she had never really felt unconditional love before and wasn't sure how to accept it. After that, we became friends, hung out, had lunch and learned from each other. Eventually, she quit drugs, got married, had a kid and found her worth. First, she had to risk coming awake to her value. You and I don't have to be fancy, or have the right words to make a difference, we just need to care and recognize worth.

Waking Up Exercises (Some tips on how to move toward empowerment):

1.   **Make a chart.** At the top put two headings: Costs and Benefits. On the left side of your chart list at least two things you are supposed to do but have been putting off . Under the Costs heading, write down the consequences of not doing what you are supposed to. Under the Benefits heading write down the benefits of doing what you have been putting off. Now weigh the costs against the benefits. Are the benefits worth the costs?

2.   **Think of some persons or person you have been avoiding.** Figure out why you've been doing that. Using the same chart you made above, list your reasons for not seeing that person under the "Costs" heading. Now think of some good reasons for seeing that person. List those under the "Benefits" heading. Take a close look at your costs-benefits ratio, and decide whether or not to call that person. Try applying the "Cost-Benefits" approach to other avoidance areas of your life. Such an approach may not keep you from avoiding someone or something, but it will at least give you a clearer understanding of the costs and benefits of what you are doing. And if the benefits outweigh the costs, you should have a pretty good idea what you ought to do.

SECTION II

GETTING RID OF THE DRY ROT

CHAPTER 3:

ENERGY DRAINING FORCES, PART 1
(Focusing on Our Negative Lacks)

"Termites are invading. Exterminate the problem. Don't eradicate the person."

Negative energy means just that, people. It's taken away from the energy we have to do good and make our lives worthwhile. Negative energy is made up of those ugly obsessions that harm our very foundations, just as much as termites harm a house. Let's take a look at a few of the biggest energy drains, and try to see them for what they really are in our lives.

Negative energy takes away from our ability to make our lives worthwhile.

Lack of Forgiveness

Let's go back to when we were little kids. Most children judge the world on a scale of right and wrong, fair and unfair. We learn very young to expect, if not demand, what is fair. How many times did we accuse a parent of saying or doing something to us that wasn't fair? Maybe your sibling got a bigger portion of food, or received something you felt you didn't. Those incidents left you with feeling of betrayal or rejection.

Many of us carry this learned sense of right and wrong into our adult life. Some of us have not practiced or even learned empowering responses to unfulfilled expectations. Instead, we respond to someone's failure toward us from our "fairness" point of view. When wronged, an immediate wall starts growing around our "soft tissue." We harden and focus intently on the fact that we've been wronged or betrayed, and we cut off our ability—and even our desire—to understand the circumstances of one who wronged us and find it impossible to

We cut off our desire to understand why someone might have done something to hurt us.

extend compassion.

Some of us become experts in judgment and burning bridges. We really believe deep inside that to forgive a wrong, to really forgive it, means validating a wrong by sanctioning it. If I forgive this person, I will become less of myself. Many people have carried unforgiveness for a lifetime, building it to monumental levels of bitterness. Unforgiveness cultivates a life-style of blame. Unforgiveness causes a warped perception of reality in the unforgiving person.

Deep inside, the unforgiving person has a frail identity that does not know its worth and has not drawn nurturing experiences from the inner self. They have succumbed to one of the giving-up seductions that cause us to define our worth and self-confidence by what others think of us.

Remember, your worth and power lies outside the domain of life's circumstances, pleasures and pains. You are who you are and can become better as you will it.

Unforgiveness is one of the deadliest energy drains there is. It's like a leak in your central heating system that leaves your house cold and unpleasant. It is ruthless and if left unchecked will freeze you right out of your house.

For decades forgiveness has been a tainted and difficult subject to explore. Much of the popular mental health movement teaches people to focus so much on the power within, the God within, the child within, and endless hidden trauma within, that the patient thinks they must focus on nothing but their own losses, betrayals or distortions. They are taught to sever ties with those who have hurt them. People, we must focus on the core person within, so it can reach without.

Not only is the act of forgiveness avoided like the plague, but the vulnerable inner self is often taught in therapy that it shouldn't forgive and extend compassion. After all, if someone has the power to forgive,

You can WILL yourself a better way of being.

that person also has the power to heal (and the healed or whole person no longer needs therapy).

It is possible to forgive while establishing appropriate boundaries, taking care of oneself and operating from insight. Forgiveness is not weakness. It is not validation of a crime or wrong doing. It is an internal acknowledgment of the life-affirming act of compassion. It is a frame of reference that recognizes that as we have needed forgiveness from others for our ignorance, selfishness or meanness, we too, recognize the universal truth that all humans err. We all need grace and compassion to survive the trials of our own failures.

Note of caution: To forgive does not mean you automatically trust someone who has hurt you, nor should it. It does not negate the reality of accountability, law, and justice. But what a difference in one's life a little forgiveness can make!

The Path Of Unforgiveness And Energy Drain

Cleaning out your house means making room for you and your preferred company. What you don't want to do is dump all the toxic waste in your front yard so it can creep back into your house. You want to take any attitudes, behaviors, habits, and distortions about your worth and capabilities and throw them a country mile. Here are some household clues letting you know where your energy and power is getting wasted.

Unforgiveness Lane One

(Home of the Killer Termites)
1) Lack of Understanding
2) Lack of Compassion

3) Lack of Tolerance

Lack Of Understanding

I have found that when I stop asking questions and stop trying to understand the world of another person, I have blundered onto a negative path leading to unforgiveness. **Part of the act of forgiveness is taking the time to seek understanding about the person who wronged you.** What stresses have they had to face in the past and currently? Were they really out to get me, or did I get in the crossfire, while they were self-destructing? Do they feel worthwhile? Are they hurting? Have they been betrayed? Could they benefit from forgiveness?

Again, you are not condoning abuse because you forgive someone. You are repairing your inner self, taking your real power back, while offering the opportunity of healing and personal revelation to a broken inner self. **Seek understanding regarding yourself and others. It will fuel your inner self and empower you in every way.**

Fear thrives on the unknown; it loses its power through understanding.

Lack of Compassion (reflects lack of understanding)
"So you tripped on the mess in my driveway.
Sorry, but you should have watched where you were going."

In order to develop your ability to extend compassion, you must seek understanding. One does not go without the other. Lack of compassion is a direct result of lack of understanding. Remember, the world is a hospital for needy inner selves, not a sanctuary for saints. We are all searching and in the process of learning from our failures.

Compassion is the healing compound that we all possess and can give in abundance. It feeds our inner selves, while

Compassion feeds the inner self while offering healing for others.

It finally became plane to Frank that he could love Lois even if her head wasn't tall.

offering healing to others.

I have seen the affects of compassion throughout my life.

One time, not long after my bankruptcy, I took the car I borrowed in to get the oil changed. While there, I was told that the noise I had been worried about was a serious and potentially expensive problem. I remember standing there and wondering what to do. I had no money and had to leave town that night for a meeting. I called a few mechanics, but none could get me in.

A few minutes later as I was pondering what to do next, a man I recognized from years ago approached me. He had been a client of mine seven years before when I was an alcohol and drug counselor. He said, "Laurie, you treated me with compassion and respect years ago when I was in treatment. I want to fix your car now." I wanted to cry, I was so touched. He ended up fixing my car (which took several hours) for free, and giving me $20.00 gas money for my trip. It felt like I had been handed a million dollars. Someone from my past had permanently contributed to the healing of my broken heart.

> Investing in compassion is investing in your own future.

Lack of Tolerance

> *"Just send them all to an island where those weird, oddball types belong."*

When you distance yourself from understanding and compassion, you move toward intolerance. You become more and more a "rigid identity" of the type described in Chapter 12. You begin to distance from your true self and buy into a giving-up program that protects you from the pain of self-discovery by building rigid personality structures and values. You have little or no patience for mistakes and differences in others and yourself. You set up black and white rules that foster self-avoidance. You may feel a momentary artificial sense of power as you chide others for their failures, but the resulting

Bill, void of compassion, plans to sue "Arms are Us."

guilt you feel punishes you for your intolerance.

Remember the two key benefits obtained from giving up are 1) sedation of the truth, creating distance from your pain; and 2) self punishment, which reinforces the self-destructive program in your deepest feelings and beliefs about yourself and life.

How many people act out intolerance on a grand scale? They promote prejudice, hate and violence towards others who live differently from them. Remember, that intolerance builds up a wall of self-deceit as a means of self-protection. Anyone who acts in a liberated fashion threatens the fragile domain of the intolerant person.

Waking Up Exercises (**Some tips on how to move toward empowerment**):

1) **Put yourself on a daily program of awareness building,** and identify ways you can practice compassion and understanding. Understanding grows when you ask questions about one's experience. Stay away from assumptions and resist the temptation to fill in the dots. Most intolerant people rarely have a truthful answer about another person's reality. Answers based on distortions and generalities are rarely based on truth. Seek truth with understanding and free up your inner self for empowerment. We all benefit from tolerance.

2) **Just as you may have become skilled at judging or lashing out, develop a quickness to offer the healing power of patience and understanding**. Lash out with a caress. Be quick to extend understanding. It's contagious once you get started. For the next week consciously stop every time you start to act intolerantly. Instead, act compassionately toward that person. Ask yourself, what angered or *threatened* you. Then

tell the person of your initial response and explain your desire to find out why the person acted as he or she did. Keep a diary in which you describe these events.

Harry and Zelma have a family discussion.

CHAPTER 4:

ENERGY DRAINING FORCES, PART 2
(Focusing on our negative mind sets)

"It was so drafty that all the heat got out."

In the previous chapter we looked at some "lacks," some energy drains from our house—lack of forgiveness, compassion and tolerance. In this chapter we'll look at some more energy drains, energy drains that can leave our house all but unlivable.

Unforgiveness Lane Two (The Killer Termites Open The Door To The Carpenter Ants)
1) Judgment 2) Bitterness 3) Hate 4) Self-destruction
Judgmentalness

The practice of judging oneself and others is as common in our lives as sour milk and stale cookies—and about as tasty. **You and I don't have to look far to find its effects. Often times we only have to look in the mirror.** I have searched my heart in this area and have found numerous examples of how I have judged others without a thought as to the damage I might have caused. Somehow, we get into a habit of backstabbing, as if it were a sport. Some of us have advanced to Olympic status. It becomes fun and offers a warped sense

Backstabbing provides a warped sense of power.

Mr. Thompson hears unforgiveness in Mrs. Thompson's voice.

of power, as we cut others down.

It builds up the fragile walls of our weak ego. "I feel magically more powerful because of the feelings of control offered in judgment. I am judge and jury. And you are not." There, Laurie has spoken. Now let's have a moment of silence and contemplate how awesome I am for tearing another person to shreds.

True judgment is a product of reasoning. It is a person's considered opinion and is usually the result of a desire for truth, understanding and justice. Our legal system must act as judge at times or there would be chaos. But it can never really be perfect. **Only God is the perfect judge because only God is perfect**. God is the perfect balance of love, compassion, understanding and fairness. What person has all those attributes? No one I know. Therefore, we just don't qualify to do God's job.

Only God is perfect and therefore only God is really capable of judging.

Judging others is hurtful to its intended target and often destructive to the one judging. It makes us less of who we are and reveals the frailties of our identity.

I have made a goal for myself. I am actively working on increasing my awareness of when I judge and whom I tend to judge. One thing I am really watching in myself is the sneaky, socially acceptable way I judge others. For instance, what kind of jokes do I tell? Do I have to slam a group or person to be funny? Wow. I have had to really work on my cynical, theatrical side that is attracted to negative humor.

Remember, I am,but GOD IS. That is the correct proportion.

I am writing down my daily successes and failures in these areas and asking God to make me a more loving person. Let's not continue to kid ourselves about what judging is—it is deceitful behavior that belittles us.

When I was a young woman just out of high school, I had a chance meeting with a man I have never forgotten. I have also never forgotten what that meeting taught me.

His name was Billy. When I was 18 I had gone to L.A. to convince Capital Records to sign me for a record deal. Surely, they would recognize talent and dedication. **Earth to Laurie. Earth to Laurie. Anyone Home?** Can you imagine them not wanting to see me? It was the first time I had left home alone on a big adventure. Of course once Capital Records refused to acknowledge my stardom I had two weeks of time to kill. I was sleeping on the floor of a friend's house. So...there I was in Santa Monica, walking up and down the streets full of used book stores and very weird looking people.

Suddenly, I noticed this frightful looking, dirty, huge, messy-haired black man lunging out from behind the alley at people walking by. He would wait till their back was to him then growl and yell like an animal, hoping, I guessed, to scare them. Some would promptly run away, some swore at him and others just ignored him. I found myself fascinated and so curious as to what would possess him to act that way.

I felt sad as I walked into a nearby grocery store to get a yogurt. I couldn't get his desperate acts out of my mind. As I walked out of the store, I was surprised to see him sitting on a newspaper rack. I would have to walk right by him, so I knew he would try to scare me as soon as I walked by. Sure enough, the moment I was five or six feet from him he roared like an animal. I decided to call his bluff, turned around, extended my hand and introduced myself.

"Hi, I couldn't quite understand what you said, but I am visiting in town. My name is Laurie Roth, what is yours?" The shock on his face was priceless. He was utterly speechless for a while until he said, "You must be very lonely to talk to me."

I told him I was bumed, almost broke and really hungry. Then I asked him if he would have a hamburger with me? So, there we were, the next TV sitcom walking into a hamburger joint—me in my conservative business suit and him looking like a crazy black Conan with corkscrew hair. Though people pointed and stared, we had a wonderful conversation. A few times when he started to act what I thought was insane (laughing incoherently) I asked him to stop acting crazy when he wasn't. Do you know he did! We talked, deeply, about his past, about rejection from his girlfriend, about his poverty and pain.

We shared into the night, had dinner on a lawn and felt a connection that is hard to describe other than two souls touching one another. We cried together and we talked about God and dreams. Finally, he turned to me with tears in his eyes and said, "I have never met a woman like you—thank you for caring for me. You can't know how much this has meant to me." We hugged, said good-bye and wished each other well, as he started to hitch-hike back toward his home in Texas. He was going to finish his goal of becoming a mechanic. I was going to keep trying in the music business. Someday someone would listen to me.

That chance meeting gave me the opportunity to share love and understanding with someone. And it showed me what giving of yourself can mean to someone else. And to you yourself. By giving to Billy I gave to myself a whole world of greater understanding.

I've known many a person who at the hardest time in their life came up with an ingenious invention or idea to re-create their reality. They knew they were down but more importantly, they knew the golden secret of success. They knew that the core of who they were still existed and they took the time to be **AWARE** of all their internal resources.

Resist the temptation to waste more energy attacking yourself for struggling with judgmentalness. Most of us do. What's done is done. Forget it. But begin checking your impulse every time you start to judge someone.

Let's show "good judgment" and love one another.

Earlier we explored the drain of unforgiveness. Unresolved unforgiveness will eventually grow into bitterness.

Bitterness

"They had taken nearly everything in my house,
but I still had my rage.
I would never give them that."

Unchecked judgment breeds a bitter spirit. **Bitterness is the fruit of truly giving up on yourself and others**. It is the final act in the drama, after repeated negative rehearsals. It is fueled by lack of understanding, lack of compassion, unforgiveness and judgmentalness. It is a parade of all your self-loathing qualities.

Anyone who looks can see its bitter expressions. It may look like violence, alcoholism, abuse, crime, rigid rituals, isolation, mental illness or physical illness. Bitterness can take on numerous forms, but all are designed to reinforce your sense of worthlessness and the worthlessness of its target. People who refuse to forgive will eventually focus so much on their "painful event" that it resembles King Kong in size. It now demands most of the energy they have.

If bitterness is your chosen way of being, you have no permission or time to heal, because you have constantly to feed your bitterness. It needs you; you become its care giver and slave.

To maintain bitterness, you must sell a part of your house. That is the only way you can pay for its insatiable demands. Why sell your own power? Remember the truth about forgiveness. You do not become less or condone a wrong by extending

> Bitterness is the sum of negative behaviors, lack of understanding, compassion and forgiveness.

> Bitterness consumes a person, body and soul. Forgiveness purges your heart and gives it room for growth.

forgiveness. Instead you purge and clean out much needed room in your heart so you can grow and claim your empowered destiny. If it is not possible or appropriate to forgive someone directly, you can certainly pray for them and give your burden (as a child would) to a loving God.

Once when I was down on my luck and myself and was acting out in rage and pain, I noticed something. Because I was honest about those gut feelings and failures, I felt compelled to the next step of healing, the step is where many of us stop. I reminded myself of the universal guiding principles of truth and justice: "You sew what you reap." "God is faithful, even when people are not." " I do not understand why suffering happens, but I know my future is in God's hands." "All people can fail sometimes." "Do unto others as you would have them do unto you."

Once I had ministered these wonderful, liberating principles of life to my embittered self, I received the energy and ability to go on. I began to humble myself before God and my friends. I recognized, not just the ways I had been violated but also the ways *I* had violated myself and others. I began asking forgiveness for my judgmentalness and bitterness. Only then, did I have enough space in my heart to pray that my enemies would find truth and empowerment in their lives. I now feel like a freshman in the school of personal liberation.

Amazingly, through these acts of humility and honesty, healing and energy blossomed. My abusers became distant and powerless. I was more concerned with my house than theirs.

Hate

Let's review the path that leads to hate. We need to recognize ways we lead ourselves to this poison water. The first thing we did to develop hate was to cease the pursuit of understanding. Bad choices after that all led to hate.

1) Lack of understanding

      Path a: Will you seek understanding?

      Path b: Will you not?

2) Lack of compassion

      Path a: Will you practice acts and attitudes of compassion?

      Path b: Will you not?

3) Lack of tolerance

      Path a: Will you exercise tolerance with others?

      Path b: Will you be intolerant?

4) Judgment

      Path a: Will you continue to judge others and yourself?

      Path b: Will you stop judging?

5) Unforgiveness

      Path a: Will you forgive yourself and others?

      Path b: Will you choose not to forgive?

6) Bitterness

      Path a: Will you celebrate bitterness?

      Path b: Will you give it up?

7) Hate

Path a: Will you continue to hate?

Path b: Will you extend love?

Hate has only one consequence: Self-destructive Behavior.

When you reach the point of self-destruction, you have to make a choice. Which path are you going to take?

Path a: Will you continue to self-destruct, while destroying others?

or

Path b: Will you heal and build a healthy identity?

It's as simple as that.

Feeding the fire of hatred means you have allowed the consumption of your own spirit. Hate demands all the energy you have. It thrives on your choice not to seek understanding or apply compassion and forgiveness. Hate is the ultimate "terminator." Its job is to seek and systematically destroy all in its path. It is the complete opposite of all that is good, true, and loving. Civilizations have ceased to exist, families have been lain to ruins, and hopes and dreams have been sold for one dark moment in hateful glory.

In order to celebrate hate, you must become as God in your own eyes. You are judge and jury. You assume the right and authority to kill: with words, with rumors, with violence, with silence, indifference, slander, intolerance—and I ask you, Who is it you are really killing?

Waking Up Exercises (Some tips on how to move toward empowerment):

1. I challenge you to defuse the destructive power of judgment by being quick to notice the good in others, to seek understanding and to look in the mirror of truth. For the next week every time you start to make a snap judgment about some-

one, ask yourself internally—Do I know the circumstances of the person I'm judging? Have I tried to understand why this person may be doing the thing that is causing my negative judgment?

2. Listen closely to the content of your conversations over the next week. How many times do you get caught in the judging trap? See if you find yourself making comments such as this: "She's really great, but, have you heard this about her?" One of the most common judging games there is, is to say something nice about the person, then slam them with some judgment or gossip. The real intent is never the compliment, only the slam, to get a reaction from the listening party. Ask yourself, "Am I guilty of this?"

3. If you find yourself making negative judgments, try correcting them on the spot. Tell the person you were starting to judge what you were doing. Say something like, "You know, I really get angry at myself when I find myself making judgments without really knowing what I'm judging. I found myself making a judgment about.... Forgive me, for that, will you? Do you mind talking to me?"

4. Think about something you hate. Write down what it is about it that you hate. Then ask yourself these questions:

   a. How well do I understand the reasons for my feelings?

   b. What are those feelings?

   c. Am I being as understanding as I could be?

   d. Am I being intolerant?

   e. Am I making unfounded judgments?

   f. Can I be more forgiving in this situation?

g. Is the bitterness I feel because of this worth it?

Is the hatred worth it?

CHAPTER 5:

DON'T GIVE UP

(Avoiding the seductive choices)

"The house seemed to close in around me, so I hid in the mess."

Many of us have been conditioned to give our power away to specific events. We all have unconsciously established what our "last straw" is. We've decided the last moment of hardship or failure we will accept before we choose to give up—before we accept the notion that we can no longer cope, solve problems or take any more, **period!** That's it!

When we decide to give up—often because we failed ourselves or someone else failed us one too many times—we usually attempt to avoid pain in more and more harmful ways, getting ourselves into a re- volving door of torment. **Some of the giving-up responses are addictive behaviors—promiscuity, restlessness, ongoing depression, rage, violent behaviors, insanity, physical ill- ness and obsessive working.**

Promiscuity, restlessness, depression, rage and other violent behavior, even physical illness are often "giving up" behaviors..

During the last few years of my "pressure cooker" recording art- ist life, I had several of my friends say to me, "I don't know how you do it. I would have gone insane after the first betrayal, let alone the bom- bardment you took. I don't know how I would have coped!" While I was on that stage I didn't know how I was going to cope either.

Sometimes I felt such rage that I would shake involuntarily at the oddest times. Sometimes the feeling of rage and pain would come through me out of nowhere, like a lightning bolt, leaving me breathless and shocked at the intensity. They would sometimes occur in the most ex- traordinary places—in the kitchen, while driving to the store, while try-

ing to sleep, while doing almost anything. Along with the feelings of rage were haunting messages and accusations that would repeat over and over again, as if I were stupid and needed to have the same message shouted at me eternally!

Why is this happening, God? How could my love relationship have failed after all this time? How could my backers have deserted me? How can my business fail when I tried so hard? I thought if you worked hard and meant well you wouldn't fail! Along with the painful *how* or *why* questions came the anger and painful statements I continually turned on myself: "You're nothing but a failure, Laurie." "It's only a matter of time before you will fail again, so why try?"

On and on the negative assaults continued. Life became a continual struggle. I dangled on the edge of giving up, contemplated its outcome, fought and fought against the convincing seductions of self pity, isolation and depression.

As my losses seemed to feed on each other—loss of personal and corporate support, loss of my best friend, loss of my long-term love relationship, loss of my 20-year recording artist dream, bankruptcy, eviction, and failing health—shock turned to rage and then transposed itself into extreme pain and grief. Except for the endless hours I spent trying to solve many of my very real problems, I isolated myself and sought compassion and healing from myself and God. I wanted to pray, but pain rendered me silent. I felt smothered by grief, transfixed by my own agony. Often, my friends' attempts at sympathy felt like cold intrusions. I was alone in the most silent agony I had ever experienced.

Slowly, I began to understand that pain has its own pace, language and intensity. Experiencing pain over so many months at such an intense level brought me to a point of painful awareness: At this point in my life, I simply had to begin providing myself the dreaded answers to the tearful questions I had been asking myself.

But then I felt an all but overpowering need for sleep, a place of
no feeling, a place to hide from my fears, from my uncertainties, somewhere I could avoid facing the answers about my suffering. The reason
I was so terrified to really get honest with myself was that I knew that
honesty would demand an almost total change in my life. It would mean
giving up the way I had looked at things. It would mean questioning the
reasons so many of my dreams had failed.

Pain has its own language, pace and intensity.

The Drifting Away Phase At this period it is often easy to begin drifting away from yourself. That process is subtle. **Often times, our self-
sabotage programming ushers forth all kinds of cues, alert-
ing us that we are in the "drifting" phase of giving up**. If
you have not armed yourself with the habit of honesty and are not ad-
dressing the needs of your identity, you may find yourself being swept
away and floundering without a foothold. Red alert!

Relationships are more precious than careers.

Learning to understand the process we go through in giving up
can strengthen our resolve *not* to give up. Watch out for signs of the
following. Think of them as red alerts, clues to alert you to get back to
your own identity, your *real-self* building program.

RED ALERT 1: **You stop taking the time to slow down.** Ironically, when
our lives are in a healthy rhythm, we take the time to rest, meditate or
pray and sit quietly in order to focus things. Slowing down enough to
maintain these experiences is food for the soul and gives our body the
energy to attend to the joys and demands of life's pressures. It is when
we feel that there is no time to slow down, no time for prayer, for intimacy, quiet reflection, family and relaxation that we end up having even
less time for work or personal things. Time seems to evaporate, though
we hurry more and more.

Remember the paradox: *Slow down to speed up.* Slow down and feed your inner self in order to have more energy and time. If you do nothing but increase your business level, you will never have enough time for anything and end up feeling restless and exhausted.

RED ALERT 2: You start feeling compelled to talk negatively about others.

Finding "dirt" on someone else is a way of avoiding finding it on ourselves.

This process is something our society supports and models, but it is a sick, dead end. It drains what energy we have for a momentary perk of "one upping satisfaction." Remember, feeling the need to find dirt on someone else is but another diversion from the need to look at the dirt on ourselves. Rather than giving into the "trendiness" of bad-mouthing someone, recognize this as a form of self-betrayal, a red alert sign of drifting away from your best self. The truth is, an empowered person, who knows their worth, does not need to tear down others, to build their inner self.

RED ALERT 3: You feel a need to establish "an enemy" to blame for your problems.

If we can convince ourselves and others that someone or some force "made us do it" or gave us license *not* to do it, we can take away the "sting" involved in peeling off one of those protective layers we've built up over our real selves. We do not have to take responsibility for ourselves. The more we campaign to *blame* the Government, God, family, employers, neighbors, Satan, race, sex, genetics and so on the more we excuse ourselves from blame. These outside forces steal our peace of mind and we lose our real identity.

RED ALERT 4: You start feeling restless and confused.

Okay, I am guilty. Everyone occasionally feels uneasy or restless, but when it descends like a cloud of chaos, robbing us of our ability to relax or focus on what we want to, then we have a problem. Feeling

51

restless is like a fly on a wound or a constant itch you can't get to. It builds a sense of anxiety and the feeling that you can't get anything done. We find we have to hurry to do everything. We end up short circuiting and accomplishing little. So many of us work so hard and feel so little satisfaction!

Restlessness is a sign that we've joined the "hurry up and do nothing" club. We run fast around the gerbil wheel, so we can run fast around the gerbil wheel. Can we all say a collective *Da!* Being restless is a signal to let us know we have driven onto the race track without servicing or gassing up our car. It is a message telling us to sit down, take a deep breath and take inventory of the important people and areas of your life.

> Restlessness is a sign to take inventory of what really matters to you, especially the important people and areas of your life.

RED ALERT 5: You let go of personal disciplines that enhance the quality of your life.

When we start letting up on any *real life-building* attitudes or behaviors, that's a sure sign we're caught in the "drift net" of giving up on ourselves. We may notice the following: Personal hygiene becomes less important (we now are preoccupied with focusing on inner negative feelings and starting the process of self-sabotage). We barely have enough energy to get out of bed, let alone slap on some make up or shave. We find it is easy to pull away from friends and functions. Finally, we stop meditating, praying and feeling appreciation for what we have. Things just seem all bad.

RED ALERT 6: You have the feeling that you are starting to set yourself up for failure and don't know how to stop it.

I have heard many clients and friends over the years state that they see ways they are short circuiting themselves, but for some reason feel compelled to continue. This process is very real. Because the system of negative self-belief is beginning to be challenged, it mobilizes its own creative army, surveys all the vulnerable areas in our lives and seeks to fulfill the commands that we gave it earlier on. It fights us. Unconsciously, we are at war with ourselves.

RED ALERTS 7: You start experimenting with "addictive" substances.

Remember, addictions can be hard to recognize at first. If we look closely we can see the signs: mood swings, increased restlessness, irritability, depression, making poor choices regarding nutrition and hygiene, giving up on meditation and prayer, letting go of disciplines, spending money you cannot afford on the addiction, increasing attempts to control others and events, bursts of rage, being manipulative and dishonest with workers and family, having credit and legal problems and having health and intimacy problems.

When you notice a few of these behaviors in yourself, watch out! You may be drifting toward chemical dependency.

RED ALERT 8: You withdraw emotionally and start hiding behind, "I don't know and I don't care".

It takes raw courage to trust the answers we get from deep inner probing.

A sure sign that we have sought a place of hiding and stopped growing is when we give into complacency and seem to be in a gray fog. We convince ourselves that if we shut off our feelings, we can drift ever further away from things that hurts. Strangely, this is a power trip. Many times one of the payoffs to shutting down emotions is the sense of power we feel from controlling the responses of others. Numbness can act as an artificial power base creating surface forms of attention from those around you.

WAKE UP TO THE RED ALERTS

The seduction of giving up gets even stronger the more honest we begin to be with ourselves. It is at this most critical time in suffering that the essence of our very being is challenged. To survive we must confront the layers and complexities of truth. It is easy to understand why people choose almost any kind of avoidance of such a personal confrontation. It takes raw courage to trust the answers we find when we question ourselves honestly.

As we begin to find the courage to answer those questions, we come to the hardest ones of all: What part did I play in the failure? Did I manage things poorly? Did I do enough research? Did I...fail? And if I failed, was I worthless? Was I even worth the effort of trying again? If I accept the failure, how can I possibly forgive myself and make things right?

Does the healing part of pain hurt as much as the grieving part? It sure did for me. But it was then that I realized that I was coming alive and aware, maybe for the first time. At that moment, I felt that I had more wealth and success than in all the years I had struggled so hard to be successful.

The real truth was, and is, we are all successes from the day we were born. Success is not some event you arrive at. It is the acceptance and enjoyment of the present. It is the dance of living, breathing, trying and retrying, experimenting, dodging, forgiving, loving and simply getting up everyday and getting on with things!

How we respond to ourselves and others in relation to hardship gives us deeper clues about where we are in our own personal awareness.

Waking Up Exercises **(Some tips on how to move toward empowerment):**

1. **Have you been experiencing a few of the red alerts?** If so, jot them down on a piece of paper. Contact a friend and tell her or him about them. Have they, too, noticed some of these behaviors in you?

2. Interview the most empowered , fulfilled person you know. Ask about their daily routines, rituals, personal beliefs; ways they achieve their goals and maintain stability. Then compare your habits, attitudes and daily routines with theirs.

3. Make a conscious decision not to give up on the important people and areas of your life. Make reminder stickers about your resolve, and put them up all around your home and work space.

4. **Redefine** *give up as*
   - give = give more of yourself in areas that count
   - up = look up to things not down on them

Now you can give and go up!

CHAPTER 6:

DON'T EXCHANGE THE PAIN

(Avoiding addictions)

"There in the rubble I saw all that was left of the TV game room."

Some habits we interpret as safe are really just ways to sedate pain and fear. And they're alluring. Addictions campaign for themselves relentlessly. Eating disorders, alcoholism, drug addictions, sexual compulsions, on and on: These are the evil politicians of the psyche that look for the weak souls who are contemplating giving up or submerging into a drugged sleep.

Let's take a look at some of the more attractive lures into self-deception.

Dependency

Over-dependency on others can be an addiction, a form of drugged sleep, another way of avoiding fear and pain. Healthy love relationships involve mutual sharing and giving. Both parties are allowed to grow and celebrate their uniqueness. However, over-dependency seduces us with a powerful sleeping drug that turns us into a "slave self." Before long the only part of us left begins to try to suck life and experience from the one we are dependent on. No one can stand this kind of dependency for very long. But in our drugged sleep, we may not recognize the destruction that is occurring in this relationship.

Dependency is but an exchange of pain.

The darkness of drugged sleep is an unconscious breeding ground for long- term pain and rage—about losing our real self, rage about not finding out the truth about ourselves and about being violated by ourself and others. We eventually awaken from our drugged sleep to the violence of a long suppressed rage that we turn it on ourselves and others around us.

Trying to find normal, peaceful sleep then becomes much harder, and the risk of looking inside much more painful because we have missed so much of our *real* life.

Fake I.D.

Dependency on others is one way of giving up our identity. Another more subtle way is to desperately attempt to merge ourselves in causes, find identity in gangs, churches or other social organizations— or simply as workaholics. We may have fought noble causes with the fervor of Joan of Ark, but for those of us who believe we are really worthless, such worthwhile activities are little more than hiding places, where we can avoid our feelings of worthlessness. If nothing else, these activities allow us to become holograms, imaginary selves, that seek approval or sympathy from a group or identity from a cause, while we hope that others do not find out just how empty and scared we really feel.

All of the above ways of hiding from are real selves are pretty obviously just that, escape behaviors. But they are not the only ones. There are other subtle but no less damaging ways of escaping from our real everyday needs.

Submerging ourselves in the stories of others is a socially acceptable way of escaping our own problems.

We can avoid ourselves quite successfully by being glued to the TV or by watching the lives of others in exchange for our own life. How interested are we really in the gossip and lives of people we see before us? Do we put that much attention and curiosity towards ourself? Submerging ourselves in the stories of others can be one of the most beautiful seductions of all. It seems to fall within social boundaries and is quite fun and entertaining. The only problem is that this mindless activity detours much needed energy to develop ourselves.

Weakness in Numbers

The third alluring part of the self-deception game is that segment of the self-help movement that says up to 90 percent of our population is diseased, dysfunctional or co-dependent. I reject that notion. We have the power and ability to wake up, make healthier choices and take control of our own lives.

Rather than encouraging us to wake up, realize our own power and take responsibility for our lives, some elements of the self-help movement encourage us to believe we have a disease or syndrome and should seek endless hours of self-help group treatment from others who have the same disease. Those of us who don't are said to be in denial of our dysfunction and dependency. Garbage!

While perhaps meaning well, many of these self-help groups end up making us feel less than we really are. They not only encourage and educate us in the expansive nature of our disease, but provide a forum for us to ruminate, blame, and rehearse our portfolio of disease symptoms. **Although, I am sure there are those who get help along the way, I am also quite sure this whole mentality has provided but another excuse for thousands to give up or go back into one of their escape-seeking addictions**.

Comfort Zones

One of the many seducers that try to keep us unaware of our resources is the "comfort zone." It's that part of us that fears change, avoids challenges and tries to keep us right where we are.

Trying new behaviors, taking ownership of our growth, takes energy which we have, *if*...we focus our attempt at growth from a posi-

Dr. Roth visits the Historical archives of Dysfunction.

tion of honesty. You will know in your gut if you are honestly working toward a better you, or if you are still trying to hide those scared parts that don't want to get cleaned up.

Comfort Zones can wear a lot of faces. They reflect what is familiar, what has always been done, what I am used to doing or feeling. Although, places and behaviors of familiarity and safety are not bad, when we use these to avoid the truth and to stay asleep, they become our own prisons.

It may seem strange that so many things that seem normal and may well be normal *are not* normal in certain situations. In those situations they are simply weird. People have always done weird and crazy things when they feel worthless, are in pain or are confused about who they really are. The only real way to stop ourselves from doing those weird and crazy things is to start doing things that make us feel good about ourselves. Therapy of any kind needs to help us learn how to become awake, alert to the possibilities for growth all around us.

Being awake is that state of awareness and vibrancy that embraces life and flows with it as it comes. Pain, often a process that occurs while coming awake, is a teacher and guide that leads us to the center of our selves, where we know by faith that worth is there.

Drugged sleep, on the other hand, is that stupor we seek to release us from our painful feelings. There are as many ways to give up as there are avoidance ideas to facilitate them. We have been discussing a few of them above.

> We need to work through our pain to arrive at our future reality.

To avoid these alluring escape mechanisms we need to take control of ourselves and move away from the "I have a syndrome/disease movement" to one whose credo is *"Future reality is what we make it."*

Future reality is the place we all have that houses our "best" self. It is the *dream* empowered, the successful reality of the very near future. This image of our future self merges with the present as we become more awake and willing to walk through our pain. This positive image is as close to us as our shadow, but unlike our shadow we can embrace it.

We all want and need love and encouragement when we are charting a new course. We need someone who deeply believes in our worth and ability to grow. Whether this affirmation comes through a support group or an individual does not matter. But we must be wary lest we get sucked into trendy kinds of groups that are built on labels and cannot really free us.

Learn as you grow to look at your behaviors as just that—behaviors and choices that are often made in response to pain and confusion that we have the ability to change.

Believe in the power of future reality and you are powerful.

The benefits of awareness come when we look, taste and listen. Feeling empowered and more energized comes when we take those first steps of courage. Then something great happens. We begin to expand the boundaries of *ourselves*. Just like a video game, we pass from level to level, and along the way we are getting new tools for our journey, new tokens of strength.

Everything you need will be there when you start practicing in faith the steps of growth and personal expansion. What do you have to lose? Nothing but sleep, and remember, discomfort and pain are only a temporary roadblock to personal expansion, fulfillment and joy. Don't be afraid to try!

Waking Up Exercises (Some tips on how to move toward empowerment):

1. Make a log of how much time you spend each week on movies, watching television, reading entertaining (as opposed to news) magazines, reading novels—especially mysteries or romances. Then set yourself a goal of cutting 10 percent a week off the time you spend doing each of those comfortable, unthreatening things. Make yourself spend that saved time on tasks to improve your life—tasks like looking for a new job, revising your résumé, or doing anything positive that it is hard to bring yourself to do. Do this for two weeks.

2. Now add an additional 10 percent of your time to escaping your comfort zones. Do housekeeping chores you've been avoiding. Spend time sitting alone, meditating. Make special efforts to mend some fences with friends or relatives. Do all of the things you've been avoiding doing that will make you feel good for having done them.

So, you've tried blaming your whole family tree for your problems and have run out of people to blame. Perhaps you should try Politics.

SECTION III

DESIGN THE HOUSE FOR THE NEW YOU

CHAPTER 7:

GETTING TO KNOW YOURSELF

"What a mess, trying to figure out how to put things

all back together."

S ome of us have developed strategic maneuvers designed to
keep us from facing ourselves. These attitudes can keep us in hiding

**We need the guts
to get to know
ourselves.**

from ourselves and others, while supporting our deepest fear that we are
worthless. As we discovered in Chapter 5, part of healing and getting on
with life is getting honest with ourselves. This means facing the pain
involved in healing and practicing the steps of courage it takes to peer
into the darkest corners of our house.

It is amazing how clever the human mind is. **Sometimes it
just seems easier to develop ways to keep people away from
what is really happening inside us than to risk getting honest with them and ourselves**. Over the years, I have become aware
of certain techniques in myself and others for keeping people at safe
distances. Some of these ways of avoiding real interactions with others
are learned behaviors that we are often not consciously aware of learning. These behaviors fit into behavior types I often use to identify my
clients. I group them into five different types:

a) the confused identity,

b) the rigid identity,

c) the surfer identity,

d) the blank slate identity

e) the empowered identity.

But, remember, most people are a continuum of personality traits.

I discuss each of these types in the short chapters that follow this one. Four of them are negative personality types; one is positive. But be aware that each of us has some of these characteristics in ourselves. It is only when the characteristics of one of the identity types overwhelm our personality that they cause trouble in our *houses of self*.

"What would I do in the following situations" Quiz

Following is a short quiz, just for your fun. It doesn't pretend to be scientific. But it will probably reinforce what you've already suspected about the way you handle things. You'll soon recognize that all the *a)* answers fit one personality type; all the *b)*s, another, and so on. Remember that few of us fit into the fairly rigid categories this quiz sorts out. Most of us have some of the characteristics discussed in the following chapters about personality types or identities. But for most of us those characteristics are part of a continuum of personality traits.

Remember, this is not a scientific quiz, and the identity types discussed in the following chapters describe tendencies in personalities we all have in that awe-inspiring continuum of traits that distinguish each of us from others.

On a piece of paper number from 1 to 10, and write down the letters corresponding to each of the possible responses. For each situation, choose the lettered response that indicates what you would most likely do; mark it 1; then—even though it may be very hard to do—

rate the rest of the responses: 2 for next most likely and on down to 5 for least likely.

1. If relatives showed up unexpectedly for dinner and you and your partner had other plans.
   a) Ask your partner what to do.
   b) Tell your relatives they should have called first, that you have other plans you cannot break.
   c) Act elated to see them and break the ice with humor, even though you wish they hadn't come.
   d) Feel a sense of confusion and struggle with what to do.
   e) Greet your relatives, tell them of your plans and discuss alternative plans to try to accommodate everyone.

2. Your boss wants you to work late, and you don't want to.
   a) Please your boss and cheerfully agree to stay.
   b) Say no and remind your boss of your contract.
   c) Consider staying late if the boss does certain things for you in return.
   d) Have trouble making the decision either way. Feel anxiety.
   e) Ask your boss what her/his specific needs are and then pursue a compromise.

3. You are with a friend and on vacation when you lose your wallet.
   a) Panic. Ask your friend what to do.
   b) Get angry at yourself and the situation. Hurl

insults at yourself for being so careless.

c) Cover up anxiety, and make jokes about the situation.

d) Feel confusion and fear. Feel at a loss for a solution.

e) Problem solve with your friend. Retrace steps and evaluate your financial options.

4. Your significant other tells you he/she wants to leave you after a 10-year relationship.

    a) Look for someone else to "want" you. And lessen the feelings of rejection

    b) Bad mouth your ex-partner for being such a jerk.

    c) Philosophize this away as just the way life is sometimes.

    d) Get lost in depression. Try to deaden the pain and emptiness.

    e) Find a supportive friend. Talk about feelings of pain and then make a survival plan.

5. Your significant other is asking you to make a decision about which restaurant you want to eat at.

    a) Say "I don't care. It's up to you."

    b) Say "This is where I want to eat. Let's go."

    c) Use charm and maneuver the conversation subtly toward your restaurant. For example, make up little lies about other restaurants: "Oh, I've eaten there and it's awful". Embellish the reputation of the restaurant you want.

     d) Feel frustration. Struggle with knowing what you want.

     e) State what you feel like eating and inquire as to your partner's preference. Then make a decision or compromise.

6. You have just been offered a great promotion, but it depends on your having to relocate across the country.

     a) Worry about the impact on your partner's job.

     b) Inform your friends and relatives you are leaving, and go.

     c) Use job opportunity as an excuse to escape certain relationships or other problems. Keep the real reason for leaving to yourself.

     d) Feel fear about coming to a decision. Feel threatened by all the changes.

     e) Write down the specifics of the opportunity and list your personnal goals. Discuss them with significant others then make your decision.

7. Your home has been flooded and there is serious damage.

     a) Feel panicky and unsafe. Look for security, immediate emotional support.

     b) Look for a source to blame.

     c) Minimize inner pain and hardship. Joke around and become task oriented.

     d) Feel shock. Look for emotional release and escape.

     e) Assess the damage. Ask for support from

friends and appropriate others. Clean up the mess.

8. Your Doctor warns you about your health, insisting you lose weight.

   a) Ask your partner what he/she thinks about your weight.

   b) Feel angry and judged. Ignore his advice.

   c) Ignore the real reason for your weight. Blame something.

   d) Feel ugly and hurt. Feel like a complete failure.

   e) Consider the health risks and honestly assess yourself.

9. You realize you are deeply in love with someone of another race. Your family disapproves.

   a) Fear rejection from friends and family and need to please everyone.

   b) Elope and inform your friends and family later.

   c) Create another scenario to gain sympathy *and* support from family and friends. Try *to* please them in other ways. Manipulate their feelings.

   d) Feel stuck in the middle. Struggle back and forth as to what is right to do.

   e) Recognize your feelings and share them with your friends and family. Discuss all the issues and challenges. Weigh the personal consequences against your feelings, then take the risk and make a decision.

10. You are invited to a staff party and are new to the firm. Impressions are important.

   a) Ask another employee if you look all right for this event.

   b) Dress and act any way you feel. Be original disregarding any company expectations.

   c) Socialize, act cool, know the trendy conversation expectations and mingle.

   d) Feel insecure and intimidated by the "powerful" people in the room. Pretend like you are occupied in the corner or read a magazine.

   e) Find out in advance what the purpose of the party is. Dress accordingly and try to go with a colleague.

Add up all of your points for response a); for response b) and so on. If you have 45 or more points for one of the responses a) through d), you will be especially interested in that chapter as we discuss them in this order: a) the confused identity, b) the surfer identity, c) the blank slate identity and d) the rigid identity, you will probably be especially interested in the chapter that discusses that type of personality. You will want to pay close attention to the **Waking Up** activities at the end of the chapter on the personality type you most identify with.

Scores of 35-44 in one of the categories show a strong tendency toward that type of personality.

If you score between 25 and 34 you are fairly average.

Below 25 means you are not very strongly oriented toward that type of personality.

The e) category represents the empowered identity, and the higher you score in it the easier you will find it to deal with others around you.

Just what is it about your name Little timmy that seems strange?

CHAPTER 8:

THE CONFUSED IDENTITY (CI)

"The confused person's house lacks windows to the world outside."

Confused Identities, or CIs, are the wandering spirits of life who do not know where they live. They have lived lives of confusion and surface experimentation. They do not really know who their best self is and do not feel worthy to succeed. Their confusion has been fueled by double bind messages like "Do as I say, not as I do." These destructive messages have come from "trustworthy" groups or people from their past, such as ministers, parents or other authority figures.

Confused identities blame others for their feeling of helplessness and emptiness.

Confused Identities display their confusion by taking on the victim's role, a "blaming" role. CIs blame others for their feelings of helplessness. They tend to overcompensate and feel hollow inside from their continual avoidance of personal honesty and responsibility. They have only tangled, negative internal messages to try to draw on for strength, so it is no wonder they focus most of their energy on the blaming process—blaming circumstances, others and God for their failures.

Confused identities often feel like victims.

CIs latch on to people. They project and promote anything that will encourage outside feedback and support for their shaky selves. Sadly, though the deepest needs of CIs are to know they are loved and worthwhile, the choices they make support their roles as victims and feeds their self-destructive and debasing image of themselves.

It is as if two warring factions fight inside for the confused inner person. One side seeks to give and receive love and to be expressive. The other side looks for positive signs of empowerment but often abuses any power they get.

It is not uncommon for many of us to have intricate self-sabotage networks in place that have been set up by our own subconscious need to make ourselves feel worthless or unlovable. These self-sabotage networks invade our unconscious minds where they grow in power, hidden from our direct vision and awareness. These feelings feed on our own self-loathing and self-betrayal and rob us of the energy we need for seeing ourselves honestly for who we really are.

For the CI, the battle between the healthy self and the inner feelings of self-loathing, becomes unbearable and too painful to process, so their primary goal becomes avoidance of pain. Now the CI unconsciously supports attitudes and behaviors that allow them to hide their deep feeling of worthlessness behind a life of self deception.

Thus, CIs must stay busy, invested in others or in causes in order to avoid the desperate voice of pain that continually screams at them, demanding existence and recognition. This voice of pain never completely dies out and can be faintly heard even when the CI is alone. CIs are almost always seeking ways to quiet their inner anxieties

Confused identities are like vampires and need to feed on others.

The confused identity, beyond everything else, tries to avoid pain.

Confused identities often turn to drugs of one form or another for relief from pain.

and pain, so they often turn to alcohol, drugs or other destructive diversions.

Regardless of what the forms of diversion are, they are all designed to put the confused person into a form of drugged sleep and to quiet the inner conflict. By focusing so intently on projects and others, the CI feels a temporary form of self acceptance. But this reliance on forces outside themselves puts CIs on an emotional roller coaster of conditional perks. Such a negative system offers only the conditional support from others that reinforce their mistaken beliefs that they are worthwhile only if they perform well, act right, look right or make the right kind of money. Now, the CI can feel artificially worthy without asking those deep questions about the nature of his or her own existence and without becoming personally honest.

> The confused identity's motto is "I am worthy because of what I do."

Meanwhile, back at the ranch, someone else has taken over the CI's residence and trashed it! **It would be frightful to imagine how many people have lived most of their lives avoiding the confusion within themselves and selling out for society's dog bones of conditional acceptance.** Could there ever be a bigger waste of natural resources than the waste of human potential for lack of understanding of oneself?

Many CIs live on the roller coaster of outside acceptance, never believing it will stop or that its structure is weak. When the ride suddenly crashes, the CI surveys the ruins (if he or she has the courage) and has to ask, where has the worth and meaning gone? If someone has invested in years of self-delusion and confusion, that person has two choices, giving up or waking up. And those waking-up choices made during a time of suffering are critical. Mistakes in how we handle our traumas can be devastating. But they have to be made if we're to turn our lives around.

Personal honesty and forgiveness have healing powers.

CIs have to start facing themselves. That is, they have to be willing to look long and hard enough to see an honest picture of their personal waste land, where they have failed and where their reliance on others failed them. Then, they must begin the rebuilding process, based on a foundation of personal honesty and awareness. That's a tough process, but I'll give you a few simple awareness activities at the end of this chapter to help you get started.

Working through the pain *develops* the courage to continue because then we are finally beginning to treat ourselves with *respect.* Don't wait for someone else to do it. You do it!

If you recognize a lot of the Confused Identity patterns in yourself, here are a few self-awareness techniques you can use to alert yourself you're falling into some negative patterns. Don't be afraid of new feelings and experiences. Let them fill you with new energy and internal joy!

Waking Up Exercises **(Some tips on how to move toward empowerment):**

1. When you find yourself starting to seek the advice of others, ask yourself if you really need that advice? Focus on making your own decisions, not pondering everyone else's advice. The feeling of confusion will begin to lift as you become more and more confident in making your own choices.

2. Write down your own likes and dislikes. Are there some of those likes and dislikes you think others might disapprove of? How much should that really bother you. Share these likes and dislikes with a friend, and discuss the way you *feel* others might react to them.

3. Write down how you see yourself now—emotionally, intellectually, spiritually, physically and sexually. For example, ask yourself if you really believe in God, and why or why not. Are you satisfied with the physical exercise you do? With the ways you try to stimulate your mind? Are you a feeling type of person—cry at movies, etc.—or more a thinker? Write down some questions in each of the categories above and then share your list and thoughts about them with a friend.

4. Imagine your *best* self. How would you look? Sound? Dress?

What job would suit that self? Who would you hang out with?

5. Start experimenting with moving out in new directions. You are now on the discovery trail, not the " feel lost and frightened" trail. Try new clothes. Make a point of talking to people you admire—find out all you can about what makes them tick. Try on different behaviors until you start to move past anxiety to comfort and clarity. Remember, some people are not going to like to see the new you, and they may say or do things to slow you down or stop your growth altogether. Give yourself the guts to ignore them.

6. What are your 10 top values? That is, what do you most value in yourself and others? Honesty? Loyalty? Put them in a list according to which you value most. That may be hard to do. But if you think about *why* you value one over another, it should help you learn something about yourself.

CHAPTER 9:

THE SURFER IDENTITY (SI)

"The surfer's house is as hollow as a house prop on a B movie set".

The SI avoids the truth about what's going on deep inside by floating on the surface. SIs have developed an intricate bag of tricks designed to keep themselves on the surface. They are often actors and trendy conversationalists. They are often masters at manipulation, slight-of-hand artists, jokesters, comedians, fast-talking salespeople who feel good while selling you something you don't want. Their way of avoiding the pain inside and trying to feel worthwhile is to entertain people, control conversations and behavior.

SIs believe that as long as they entertain and control others, they will be worthy and people will like them. The fact that they are skilled at entertaining and manipulation gives the surfer an artificial sense of worth and accomplishment. **The supreme challenge is tricking the public, making people believe they have it all together when they feel lost inside**. It is a false power base, one that easily gives way to the winds of adversity.

The primary motive of SIs is to avoid pain and personal honesty. Surfers dance along the waves, apparently happy, but they really feel hollow inside. They can hardly tolerate being alone because having no

Surfer identities can be con artists who try to con everyone, including themselves.

Surfers have no real base in reality.

85

stage means having no worth.

Being alone invites the giving-up-choices of substance abuse, sexual addictions and more. These various addictions are artificial highs, avoidance strategies used to try to accomplish two critical things. First, the temporary high of the preferred drug propels the surfer away from the inner pain of feeling worthless. Second, when the low comes after the high, the surfer's system of self-debasement and self-hatred is rein-forced. The *destructive force* within this identity must create failures to fuel itself and keep the *truth* about their worth in hiding.

Being alone is a painful experience for empty people like surfers.

Surfers need to understand they are really fooling only themselves. Surfers float along on the surface of life, feeding their faces with the junk foods of life. Those are addictive and they are also not very healthy. No wonder the surfer soon feels bloated with self-loathing.

Surfers need failure to reassure themselves they are worthless.

Waking Up Exercises (Some tips on how to move toward empower-ment):

1. Start spending some time alone with yourself. That's no easy task for some of us, but if you have strong surfer tendencies, just being alone and thinking about yourself is a good place to start making changes. Force your self to sit for 10 or 15 minutes a day by yourself and relax. Try to close your eyes

and empty your mind. Imagine yourself relaxing. Start relaxing your feet and legs. Feel them relax. Flow with it. Let it come up through your thighs and groin. Feel your stomach relax. Feel the pleasure of not being up tight. Let that pleasure flow up your chest and into your arms and hands. Then let it move into your head. Feel how easy you can breathe. Some people find that at this point it helps to make a little humming sound in the back of the throat and just focus on it. Try this at least once or twice a day for a week—just 10 to 15 minutes. Then pay attention to the way it makes you feel.

2. Write down your feelings about yourself. What is it you most fear in everyday life? What can you do to overcome that? What is your greatest hope for yourself? What steps can you take now to begin making that hope become you? What are your worst everyday failings? How can you overcome them? What kinds of things are your greatest everyday successes? How can you make more happen?

3. The next time you are at a social function, listen carefully to those people you visit with. Count silently to four before you reply to anything they say to you. Let silences and spaces happen—they show respect for others. Focus on building on what they have said about themselves instead of turning the

conversation to yourself. Give others the chance to become impressed with your *listening skills.*

4. For two whole days, try this tough assignment: Every time someone says something to you, paraphrase it in your own mind. Try thinking about what it really means before rushing in and trying to maneuver the conversation toward yourself. *Be Present!* Train your mind to focus on the conversation at hand instead of what you are going to say next. Once you've forced yourself to do this take stock of the way others react to you.

5. Write down your top 10 values and prioritize them. Then imagine your closest friend, and do the same for her or him. Try prioritizing them in the order you think that friend would. See if you can learn anything about your friend in the process or about yourself.

Susan this is not quite what I had in mind when I said "find a place of safety."

CHAPTER 10:

THE BLANK SLATE IDENTITY (BSI)

"I looked around my house and felt this enormous emptiness!"

The blank slate identity (BSI) feels more than anything a deep void inside. They feel empty at their core and dread looking honestly at themselves, because of the terrifying fear that they have nothing to offer. They view themselves as a stranger, housing a foreign body, always just going through maintenance "staying alive" motions. **BSIs are the people full of "I don't know" and "I don't care" statements, afraid to assert a real opinion, lest their frail ego is rejected or challenged**.

The blank slate identity feels alone and isolated from others, hollow inside-empty-and therefore worthless.

The BSI feels a kind of numbness and isolation, often caused at an early age by extreme trauma and abuse. As children BSIs were seldom rewarded for their ideas, and because their ideas were not accepted by others who were important to them, usually care givers, they began to doubt their own worth. Because experiencing real feelings and sharing real thoughts were not rewarded, BSIs sedate the pain and choose not to feel. They live in a gray fog, with their primary goal being to avoid conflict and stay safely hidden from others and themselves. Millions of people learn to perform the survival ritual. They work hard and raise families, but inside they are starving for real interactions with others.

The BSI first needs to acknowledge the real truth about their worth. Though bad things may have happened to them and people may have said they were worth nothing, the truth is that independent of how they have been treated and what they have done, they were crafted by a loving, caring God. In the eyes of God they are worthwhile.

I have a friend who lived most of her life second guessing herself and feeling worthless. She came from a loving family, yet, struggled at school. The cruel labels others tacked on her often threw her into the depths of shame and despair.

She became a fearful person. She feared change, asserting opinions and taking any kind of risks. One summer she came to live with me, and we decided to declare war on this fearful sense of worthlessness she felt. We took on the negative internal beliefs that had robbed her of her real identity.

I first began by lovingly pointing out when she was whining. I coached her daily by confronting her when she made self-demeaning or negative statements about herself. She was shocked at how often she spoke negatively. We wrote these statements down. Then I gave her some personal affirmation statements to start saying daily. "I am worthwhile and I can do anything I set my mind to." "I can and will stop focusing on those who have hurt me and start running my own race." "Today is going to be a successful and rewarding day." I also introduced her to other positive and caring people. Over the summer, she gained little bits of courage, started sharing more opinions, got a great job, lost weight, and set goals for herself. She had now begun painting on her beautiful, blank slate!

It is better to live one day with the knowledge that you are worthwhile and lovable than a lifetime of numbness and emptiness, waiting for some "movement" or person to affirm you. God has given you everything you need to be fulfilled and successful. Embrace the chance you have right now.

Here is the challenge for the BSI: Instead of focusing on the vague mess inside yourself, begin accepting yourself as a person of worth, and take responsibility for developing your own powerful identity by setting up your table with food for both your body and inner self.

When a person who feels empty wakes up and wants to become whole, to be healed, they are vulnerable to all kinds of useless inputs and treatments. You are your own doctor, so tell yourself, "Physician, heal thyself." Acknowledge hurt and disappointments straight on. Your mission is to face your pain and loss, take responsibility for your own healing, and start building your new and improved house! Do not let yourself get stuck in discouragement because of that part of your life you feel you wasted.

Waking Up Exercises (Some tips on how to move toward empowerment):

1. Think of yourself as a builder. Instead of being resentful or

numb about having no house plans, take responsibility to change that right now. You own the property and have the lumber. Start imaging what you want your house to look like, how *you* want to be—how you want to act, look, smell and *be*. Don't let others rob you of your own dream house.

2. If you don't know what you really want to be like, get out and find out. Take a walk in a public place like a mall. Look at others with an eye to seeing the way they walk, act and dress. Pay special attention to those you like. Think about what you would have to do to be like them.

3. Read about or interview people you admire. Always keep asking yourself what it is about them you find so admirable.

4. Take time to look at your values again. List 10 values important to you. Prioritize them. Which are the ones you are happy about—that is, the ones you feel you live up to in your own life? Which are the ones that need some work? Get to work.

CHAPTER 11:

THE RIGID IDENTITY (RI)

"Don't touch that! I have everything placed exactly where it should be."

The Rigid Identity has found comfort in routines, rituals, black and white thinking and stereotypes. The RI has scripted a number of *shoulds* and *should nots*, trying to build her or his own worth by taking a kind of stern parental attitude toward others. It gives them a surface veneer of stability. Underneath it all, RIs are brittle and often terrified. They unconsciously fear that if their props and rigid routines were to evaporate, they would cease to exist. What energy the rigid person has is invested in reinforcing the mythology of their black and white world. By putting so much attention on the surface, they do not have to ask the scary questions that delve deeper into the gray matter of their soul and heart. RIs fear that real understanding of their inner selves would reveal only emptiness. Because of that, RIs are very fearful of getting beneath the rigid image they project to the world. Any process that introduces colors other than black and white is to be avoided. At the core, RIs are full of pain and haven't taken the time to explore themselves. They have

RIs find comfort in routines and rituals because it gives them a sense of stability.

slipped into a giving-up program of rigidity.

These are the types of people that often make my stomach hurt. They tend to be sticklers to details without any concern for the problems they may be causing others. "I understand your report is due in the morning, but I went off duty 2 minutes ago. I'll help you tomorrow." Or, have you ever been dying for a fast food breakfast. You pull up to the driveway and the guy tells you that 33 seconds ago they stopped serving breakfast. These are not big deals, but if you have a whole country filled with people who live by the *rigid* book, it drives you over the edge! **Now imagine a lifetime of living with rigid beliefs about how blacks act or whites act, how religious people should dress or act, and on and on**. Maybe there really is a final straw that can break a camel's back!

I believe that thousands and thousands of people hide from themselves, using the pattern of rigidity. Only those who have dared to journey to the center of themselves are really able to seek understanding in themselves and others. Rigid people take pride because they have seen the detail of one tree. They fixate on the security of seeing and touching one piece of bark on one tree. They lack the inner strength to imagine the rest of the forest—or how that tree they see interacts with the rest of the forest. Because they have given up on trying to find the big picture, they will settle for the misperception that only one tree exists. This personal compromise robs the rigid person of any kind of real joy and fulfillment.

Waking Up Exercises (Some tips on how to move toward empowerment):

1. If you find a little bit too much rigidity in your own personality, remember there are all kinds of houses and all kinds of ways to keep and decorate a house. We're all different. **Try to find some strengths in those you find the most (annoyingly?) different from yourself.** List the things about that person that most annoy you. Then try to think of why that person does each of those things. How might those things support that person's sense of living a happy, fulfilled life? In what ways might they just be protective mechanisms—that is, shields to keep others from hurting them? Ask yourself if any of the things you do are those kinds of protective mechanisms? How might you change them? What kinds of things might you do to make the other person find it easier to deal with you? Easier to be with you?

2. Every time someone's behavior annoys you, ask yourself, "Why is this person doing what so annoys me?" Allow yourself to trust that

other person's process and style. View their differences as interesting, challenging and compelling, rather than threatening and offensive. See if by doing that you don't somehow feel enlarged by your act of acceptance.

3. Make a list of your most rigid behaviors and attitudes. Then try changing all of them for one whole week. Start thinking about the changes the first thing you do in the morning. Get out of bed on the opposite side (unless it means causing your mate real problems). Hold the soap in the other hand when you bathe. Brush your teeth in a different way. Eat an entirely different breakfast. You get the idea.

4. And while you're disrupting all your daily routines, make it even more tough on yourself. Every time you start to fall back on one of your rigid ways of dealing with others, don't do it. Do something so completely different that person (if he or she knows you) will walk

away wondering what in the world is going on—is the sun about to rise in the West.

5. Keep a daily log of your changes. In it monitor your own feelings and those of others as they react to you. You may just be shocked at how powerful and happy you can really feel when you teach yourself to be open and adaptable. You may even find it's kind of fun to laugh at yourself.

CHAPTER 12:

THE EMPOWERED IDENTITY (EI)

"There's an easy kind of orderliness about the house of an empowered person."

Empowered Identities are people who have faced themselves and been honest about their pain and failure. EIs realize they are successes "just because they exist" and that life is a journey of trials as well as joys. They know personal freedom because they have the freedom to choose their attitudes toward events. They know that events or people cannot rob their inner peace and knowledge of the truth about their worth. They have practiced the skill of forgiveness and developed the ability to choose their battles. Their foundation is solid and their walls are flexible. When the harsh wind blows, they hold their place and sway but do not break. RIs have nourished themselves on soul food and have extra energy to draw from. Life's problems have become the laboratory of learning opportunities and inventions, not insurmountable threats.

Life's tough challenges are the things on which we grow.

EIs feel good feelings about themselves as a result of embracing healthy thinking, practicing inner-self building experiences and caring about others. Just as we need to eat food to survive physically, the empowered person knows that they will starve if they don't feed their inner needs.

Finally, the empowered person does not let anything or anyone make her or him its slave. The EI does not submit to the seduction of helplessness from any therapeutic movement that wants her or him to go backward instead of forward. EIs instinctively know that time is precious, so they choose to make the best of it by taking responsibility for themselves. They are honest about their pain and failure, and choose to confront the truth where possible, and move forward!

Waking Up Exercises (Some tips on how to move toward empowerment):

1. What separates the EI from the other four identities. List for yourself at least three ways the EI differs.
2. Empowerment takes daily reinvestment in healthy attitudes and behaviors. We need to keep expanding and setting ever more difficult goals for ourselves. Make a list of five things that frighten you or that you shy away from doing (not dangerous, foolhardy things). Do them. Enjoy the expansion process.

SECTION IV

MOVING IN

Chapter 13:

Awareness

(Awareness of who we really are)

*"It was so much fun to walk through the new house
and see what I'd really made of it."*

Have you ever really looked at yourself? Tried to crawl inside to see what you look like inside that dark house of self with so many rooms that move off in so many directions? Have you ever taken the biggest adventure of all, "Journey to the Center of Self?"

Being aware is the first door to discovering your best self, the real you that wants to be seen. Being aware is coming awake to something that is actually you—having the courage to look, assess and give yourself a loving hug.

Coming awake is like accupressure—when we press hard it hurts from the focus and pressure; then amazingly the pain lessens and the muscle feels like new.

Awareness could be described as the art of being alive, awake, alert to the wholeness of existence. Being aware takes practice, desire to see the big picture and the will to understand its smaller more specific designs and to know how they might fit together for the day you're in. The rest is up to God.

Coming awake is like accupressure: When you press hard it hurts from the focus and pressure, but then amazingly the pain lessons and the muscle feels like new.

Become keenly aware of your personal environment.

10 WAYS TO INCREASE YOUR AWARENESS OF YOUR ENVIRONMENT

1. Awareness of Room exercise. Close your eyes, breath deeply and focus on all the sounds you can hear around you. Then try to see everything in the room with your eyes closed. Do this exercise with a friend and describe what you see and hear. Then try to describe everything you can think of about the other person. What are you aware of? What is hard to describe? What seems obvious and what feels hidden? Write down your responses. Share with each other.

2. Take a Walk exercise. Take a walk with the purpose of becoming much more aware of your surroundings. Notice sounds, smells, people walking by; register the details. Who gets close—who stays at a distance? How does your body feel, look and smell? Do you feel cautious, bold, exposed? How are you projecting yourself to the rest of the world? Next, take a walk with a friend who does the same. Afterward, share each other's perceptions about everything around you on the walk. Share with each other how it feels to increase your level of awareness?

3. Awareness of Power exercise. This time when taking a walk or going out in public, go out of your way to make eye contact with others. Smile, and share warmth. Give compliments where you can and watch what happens. Take notes again. What are you aware of internally and externally when you smile and connect with others? (Can you change your environment with a smile? You bet!)

4. Variation. Repeat the power exercise but wear clothes you normally wouldn't wear. Do your hair differently. Dress more formally or dress down. Register reactions within yourself. What are you feeling as different responses come your way? How are others reacting to a "different"

Projecting confidence gives confidence.

you? Maybe it's your posture or attitude that is different. Just projecting confidence with an upright posture can make a world of difference in the way others respond to you. Have fun!

Make your world secure.

5. Awareness of Security exercise. Take inventory of your home. How secure is it from unwanted intruders? Check windows, locks, emergency phone numbers. Take inventory of your neighborhood, and establish escape routes. Jot down who you would call in an emergency and what strategies/defenses would use if you had to?

Develop ways to ensure your personal space needs.

6. Awareness of Personal Boundaries exercise. How much space do you need around you to feel comfortable? What would you do if someone you didn't know stood one foot from you at a party or gathering? How much space do you need if you are looking for a seat in a theatre, coffee shop or class? Write down your responses. Then go out to some public gathering and pay attention to your boundary comfort zones. Discuss them with a friend. Write down three possible responses if someone stands too close. Practice nonverbal, gracious ways to move further away from another if you need to.

7. Variation. Awareness of personal boundaries. What things do others ask that make you uncomfortable? What feels like prying? Write down areas you want to keep private. Then write down intrusive questions that others ask. For example: "How old are you?" "How much do you make?" "Where are you going?" "Let me help you decide."

List these and discuss the boundaries with a friend. Strategize ways to deflect unwanted intrusions.

8. Awareness of Self exercise. Sit with a friend and write down everything that describes the other person. Share your views with each other. Then write down everything you can think of that describes yourself. Ask your friend to describe you in the same way. It is often interesting to note the differences between your friend's views of you and your views of you. Note how you feel inside about the way you and your friend describe you. Any embarrassment or concern about exposing yourself honestly? So often during this exercise we will focus on our negative or general traits. Try to look deeper for that warmth and goodness in you. It really is okay to love yourself!

> It really is okay to love yourself.

9. Awareness of Problem Solving exercise. Develop an ability to solve problems *in advance* of challenges. This way *you* have techniques for maintaining control. Remember, fear often has to do with the unknown. Let's unmask it. Write down a list of possible events that could happen, positive and negative.

> Anticipate problems so you are ready for them when they come.

For example:
1. Job lay off.
2. Illness.
3. Promotion.
4. New relationship.
5. Move to new city.
6. Divorce.
7. Start new business.

Write down your list. Then create a problem-solving strategy sheet. Planning ahead and practice always helps when challenges confront us. Write down all the possible ways you could respond to your challenge in the following categories.

Problem Solving Strategies

Response	Time	Feeling	Behavior	Plan of Action
Immediate				
3 days				
1 month				
6 months				

10. Awareness of Small vs. Big Problems exercise. Learn to accept the fact that at least 10 percent of life will annoy and disappoint you. Learn to blow it off gracefully. It is also important to separate what is really important to solve *right now*, and what can wait or be delegated out. Write down on a piece of paper every problem you can think of. Next, prioritize which must be solved first, second, third and so on. Give your problems timelines and assign problem solving strategies next to each one. Share with a friend if you wish. Try to redefine each problem as a "solvable challenge."

For example, create a chart like the one shown below. Assign your problems to those columns and put a number from 1-10 next to each problem, 1 being most critical and 10 being least. Now you can begin to see from a more objective perspective what needs attending to. Remember that you are the boss, not your problems.

Now <u>this</u> Herald, is a big problem!

Problems (1-10)

	Right Now	**Tomorrow**	**1 Week**	**1 Month**	**6 Months**
lonely-want boyfriend. (3)					x
can't pay rent (1)		x			
want to loose weight (2)				x	

Once you have a clear view of your challenges, brainstorm on another sheet of paper possible strategies to solve them. For example:

Problem 1. Lonely-want boyfriend (3) 6 month plan.

Solutions: Research organizations, clubs and associations in the area. Check library, chamber of commerce, paper and ask friends.

Establish more ways to be seen. Join more things.

Plan vacation in 5 months. Save money. Etc.

Interview friends. Ask how they met their mate.

Problem 2. Can't pay rent (1) Right now.

Solutions: Ask for 30 day extension.

Offer partial payment.

Ask friend or family for help.

Create extra income.

Get roommate.

Over the years I have heard myself and many friends say, "If

113

only I had paid attention to the pain in my side…or listened to the warning signs from my spouse…or looked at the negative crowd I was in….” But I didn't. Instead, I tried some avoidance behaviors. Now I am paying in all kinds of ways for the very acts by which I thought would avoid the pain.

When we choose to be unaware of the condition of our house, our self, we may sedate the pain temporarily, but all too quickly the cost of this pain reliever hits us like a hammer.

Coming totally awake and aware may cause us to hurt and cry, but staying in the sedation of drugged sleep can rob us of our dreams and wipe out our future.

Remember, avoidance is a choice, a choice to be unaware. And it's often a costly one.

For many of us, sitting in the dark by ourselves has become a comfortable if lonely place—a place of avoidance and soul sleep. It is a false safe haven, a very insecure stronghold. Here, we can convince ourselves that we are merely resting a moment, regrouping for the time we are ready to turn on the light and get on with living. But the truth is often that we so fear the pain of what we'll see in the light that we can't get past the thousand excuses urging us not to look, convincing us that if we do look, like Lot's wife, we will die and turn to stone.

The truth is that pain wrought from moral courage seldom kills. That pain is a life-giving force, a healing agent. It is totally unlike pain that is wrought from self-lies—that pain can breed perpetual torment and living death.

Once we have decided that in spite of the pain we will look deeply inside ourselves, we have taken the first step toward self-empowerment. *That is the first step of awareness.*

Increasing your environmental awareness will greatly enhance the quality of your life.

Avoidance is a choice, and a costly one.

Pain wrought from moral courage is a healing agent.

Once we find the courage to look inside ourselves, we have taken the first step to self-awareness.

Awareness of Distortions (Cleaning out our house)

Let's clean out the distortions in our house. Becoming aware is an investment in honesty, honesty with ourselves, others and God. When we realize that pain is but a passageway to personal fulfillment and empowerment, we gain courage. That courage grows as it endures the trials of personal honesty and awareness. And it builds the environment that nourishes our character.

Developing awareness of your best self is the same as building a foundation. If the foundation is solid, it can withstand incredible weight. It can even handle storms and cracks, maybe an earthquake or two. Even if a terrible tornado blows away our home with all its ornamentations and possessions, the foundation still stands.

People who never bother to develop an honest foundation, who fail to appraise the fullness of their identity and character, are but waiting for the moment when an inevitable storm will shake the very foundations of their existence. To be able to sustain the worst storms we must know what we are rooted to, what anchors us to the ground and still have the ability to bend with the wind. We will have sought out the weaknesses of our foundations, and figured out ways to repair them.

Often those weaknesses, those fissures, that threaten the foundation of our house are things that happen to us in early life. I remember an event of terrible pain during my high school days that caused me considerable soul searching:

Taking the time to build a strong foundation will support us, even when life throws the worst of its winter storms our way.

It was my high school prom and the music was blaring. Kids were dancing, and, of course, looking cool. I had never learned how to dance, but was dying to be asked by someone. Finally, one of my classmates, a developmentally disabled boy, came up and asked me. I accepted, *happy* to finally get the opportunity.

We were quite a picture. Neither one of us knew how to move, but that didn't stop us from trying. I was really getting into it and beginning to smile with pleasure—when the laughter started. We looked around and noticed several students, smirking, pointing at us, and even doing grotesque imitations of us. "Look, there's Laurie with the retard!" I remember the humiliation and pain I felt at that moment and wondered why their opinions meant so much to me. They shouldn't have, but they did. I remember running home in tears, angry and hurt. How could they be so cruel?

From that experience I learned how easy it is to focus on what others think instead of what the reality is. Why had their cruelty hurt me? How could a bunch of guffawing kids challenge my self-image and sense of worth?

For too many of us painful childhood and adult experiences chip away at our sense of worth, causing us to put up protective barriers. Sometimes the cost of those barriers is paid by a lifetime debit of self-worth and self-love. Some of us become forever **reactionary** instead of **actionary**. And that's an awful shame. We have to remember that *only* we control our feelings. No one can hurt our feelings without *our* permission.

No one can hurt your feelings without your permission.

If we knew how much uncultivated talent and amazing resources lay beneath our surface, we would call the nearest insurance agent and insure ourself for millions of dollars.

We've all known someone who at the hardest time in their life found some ingenious way to recreate their reality. They knew they were down but, more importantly, they somehow knew that secret that allowed them to recover and thrive. They knew that the core of who they were still existed and they took the time to focus all their internal resources, to become completely aware of the possibilities still within them.

How can we become so aware? Learn to trust ourselves? Expand our creative vision in times of distress? Only by looking honestly at what we have to work with—and then *start using it!* Knowing what we have to work with is never bad. It is almost always good. Even if we feel insecure and not very impressive, we can take little steps starting from a place of honesty. As we begin to become aware of our resources, it's as if the landscape of our life begins to color itself. We notice, color, depth and details we had not noticed earlier.

Now something truly wonderful begins to happen: We begin to see and understand relationships among all the details within our vision. This process empowers us to keep looking and trying to re-create ourselves.

Feeling kind of hollow? Kind of empty as you look inside? Afraid of what you're seeing now? Don't run now. Anxiety and pain are indications that we are getting honest with ourselves!

Congratulations are in order. We are now on that rare path to becoming fully aware human beings. With this comes all the rights and privileges of citizenship. We needn't be afraid of fear. Fear gives us the clues that help us become honest with ourselves. Fear and pain are like markers, gifts to aid us along your path of growth and personal success. We need to look at our fear, know in our hearts we are close to the truth and be thrilled for the opportunity to have the chance to know and challenge ourselves.

Waking Up Exercises (Some tips on how to move toward empowerment):

1. Ask yourself specific questions—probe yourself like a concerned physician:

    a) What is making me afraid now? List your fears from the most feared to the least feared.

    b) Ask yourself, "What is the worst thing that can happen to me if what I fear comes to pass?"

    c) In the event that scary something happened, rehearse all the possible options you would suggest to a friend who felt this way.

    d) What advice would you offer your dearest friend who faced a frightening situation, or was afraid of her- or himself?

2. Finally, practice giving the same advice to yourself and see how it feels.

    b) List your feelings.

    c) Sort them out into opposing categories such as *Enlarging—Belittling* or simply *Good—Bad.*

A lot of fear has to do with the unknown. I'd rather know what and who I have to fight and what my weapons are, than to lash out in the dark at an invisible monster.

CHAPTER 14:

GETTING TO KNOW THE NEIGHBORHOOD

"It's interesting how when you look around

there are a lot of hidden resources in the neighborhood."

I have heard many people say, "I'm not talented" or "I'm not organized" or "You're a natural salesperson and I'm not" or "I'm left brained or right brained" or "I don't have the look you do" and on and on. How often we meet people who when given any kind of opportunity find millions of excuses for not taking it? It seems like almost every day we meet people whose main script in life is, I can't, don't have the time, don't have the money, don't have the health, don't have the talent...I'm not a risk taker, I was burned once—never again... and on and on. Someone ought to write a book just on the 1001 most popular excuses for giving up!

Using excuses are often just other forms of personal sedation, often demonstrating a lack of trust in oneself. Using excuses are great "giving up tools" because they support our distorted position that we are powerless. They are often just signs that we are afraid of failing. We all sometimes need an injection of truth that reassures us that failure won't kill us, lessen our worth or rob us of our dignity. *Trying* itself is success. Failures must happen in the laboratory of personal growth and creativity. They are a natural food group in the progression of living, learning and conquering.

So we must learn to stop the excuses and **try.** The notion that we must stay away from that potential risk is distorted thinking. Few people actually want to see us fail, and the world isn't really out there plotting against us. (I am convinced, however, that *all* nylons were designed to purposely rip the minute you put them on!)

Let's talk about our potential. **Hidden within our everyday is all the evidence a jury would need to convict us of being capable of much more than we give ourself credit for**. Just because we may not have a big time job or the "right" education doesn't mean we don't already have within us many skills that could be translated to other work challenges.

One day a woman came to me saying her husband had just left her and that she didn't know how to survive. She had done nothing, she said, beside being a housewife and mother when her husband took off with another woman, leaving her in shock and fear of the future. We spent some time working through her feelings and grief. We then approached her feelings of fear and inadequacy. She said she had never worked before and had always been told by her abusive husband that she

had no skills and would never make it on her own.

I asked her if she was willing to go through the pain of getting honest and confronting the truth about herself. She said she would try. I went on to ask her more questions about her day to day routines, interests and household responsibilities. I asked her what it was like raising children, what were the highlights and the difficult challenges? How did she cope then?

After she shared with me for some time I said, "It's astonishing how such a dumb, worthless person has demonstrated the discipline and stamina of a CEO in raising children; shown the creativity of a professional artist when cooking and decorating for hundreds, solved problems on a limited budget with the efficiency of a corporate accountant and endured with the grace of a decorated soldier her position as a mother and wife".

I further said that I thought she had more collective and practiced ability then almost anyone I had ever met. She had everything she needed to conquer the world. Becoming aware of who she really was the first step; letting go of the self lies, the next step. But, finally, to keep moving ahead she needed to acknowledge her real worth and let courage guide her to the next level of growth.

Soon the life came back into her eyes as she began to glimpse the vision of her worth, and she took on challenge after challenge. One little step at a time. We began to take inventory of the dozens of skills and rusty talents she could cultivate. We exposed her dreams and interests. Then we did the research that allowed her to build an information fortress of everything she was interested in. Then came the homework and experimenting, while maintaining a support system of encouragement around her. Wow, she had become out of control. But wasn't that the point? She was without anyone's control except her own.

Remember, you don't need money to ask questions. Ask everyone you can think of questions and take notes in your mind. Information offers anyone a path to personal success and goal fulfillment. The more you know and are aware of, the more distance you can cover on your new road of empowerment.

Tips About Coming Awake

Surround yourself with positive and supportive people. If you can't find the support at home seek support at church, health clubs, support groups, etc. Don't be afraid to ask for help, just make sure the help is from someone who believes in your capabilities and worth.

Start practicing positive, awake language to yourself at home and at work. "I am going to be healthy." "I am choosing to take the steps necessary to grow and take charge of my life." "I have the God-given strength to succeed in anything I set my heart and mind to."

" I am allowed to be successful and joyful." "With God's help, I will conquer this hardship—it does not have the power or permission to conquer me."

Try experimenting. Try new behaviors. Probe yourself for fun. Do you want to change your hair, makeup, clothes and style? What did your personal style mean to you when you were more unaware of yourself and your worth? What does it say about you now?

Try creative research. Look into your undeveloped talents and interests. Libraries offer loads of current information about almost every career and interest area. Best of all it's usually free. You don't need money to grow and expand your options. Just get started.

Interview people you admire who have special qualities or who have careers you are interested in.

Develop a dream book and set goals, short and long term. Then, write out the steps and potential obstacles in your way.

Design creative solutions to combat each problem. Get a supportive friend to bounce ideas off of.

Each time you come to a wall and all you hear is "I can't," stop a minute and document what you are telling yourself and what you are feeling. Look honestly at what is in the way and try and problem solve through it. You will feel such a high as you conquer your fear.

Fear barks but rarely bites when confronted.

Read about inspiring people. Infuse inspiration into your life. Watch moving films about people who are "real" and who embrace life. Start reading about only good things. Remember, garbage in, garbage out.

Go to the zoo. Learn wisdom from the animals. Listen and watch the simplicity of their sharing, giving and loyalty.

Take a walk in the park or woods and practice breathing deeply. Start training your mind to sit and rest while breathing deeply. Relax. Tell yourself that part of doing the best you can is to refuel and rest. Let go and let God. Restlessness solves nothing.

Keep turning up the volume on your awareness button. Gifts and treasures lay at the feet of those who listen with their heart. In the upcoming chapters we will explore in depth ways to enhance and expand your energy.

Waking Up Exercises (Some tips on how to move toward empowerment):

1. Let your mind wander for a minute and write down people, hobbies and jobs you are curious about. What subjects interest you now and what interested you when you were little? Commit to researching more about your top interest areas. For example, you might interview people, read books, check

information centers at the library and on computer.

2. Develop a profile of every task you do at work and at home, starting from when you get up in the morning until you go to sleep at night. On one side of your paper list the specific behaviors you do routinely throughout the day; in a middle column list the feelings associated with each action; on the right-hand side list whether this activity involves more thinking, physical labor or other. At the bottom of the page identify the behaviors that are similar, feelings that are similar and so on.

3. Compare tasks and feelings between work and home. Now, what would your fantasy list of behaviors, routines and feelings be? What can you dare to imagine yourself doing? In one year, or two years, or ten years? Write out some hypothetical goals and proposed steps to get there. What do you have to loose? You are becoming aware of all your options.

Herb and Eunice contemplate the benefits of lying.

CHAPTER 15:

FURNISHING YOUR HOUSE

"For once I didn't have anything to hide in my house. All that was worthless had been stolen or thrown out and all that was worth keeping was on display."

Pursue Integrity In All Areas Of Your Life.

During a live "bad cop" trial on television, one police informer stated that 10 percent of the New York cops were good, 10 percent were bad and 80 percent wished they were good and honest. But the 80 percent were swayed by the need for acceptance by their fellow officers, even though those officers were corrupt. What a sad testament to the place of law in our lives—the loss of integrity at the highest level of public trust!

When I was a child I remember the comfort I felt at being taught that there were black and white values. There were truth and lies, right and wrong. It was a safe arena I could count on. I was told it was wrong to lie, cheat and steal; yet, even with loving parents and moral guidance, I remember times I lied, cheated and stole things. I tested the limits and reasons for those limits.

As a creative child I remember asking the scary questions of life. Who determines what honesty is? How black and white are honesty and integrity? Can they slide with changing times, trends and values? Or if I want something bad enough, could I lie to get it? I was challenged to find out the truth about truth.

Recently my father retired from a career as an educator and pastor. One day I remember him saying in a moment of reflection that he hadn't made much money or pastored large churches or published a best seller, but he had lived an enriched life because he loved God and had his family and his cherished dog, Angela. I remember feeling moved as I looked at him and felt his courage and the strengths of his beliefs as I never had before. I realized how proud I was of him no matter how we differed on opinions. He had loved me and been true to me, and he had not sold himself for money or power. I remember the kindness he and mom had shown all kinds of people, sometimes to their own detriment. Because dad and mom had both chosen to live their lives the way they had, they faced retirement with self-respect, new goals and empowered identities to continue living adventure after adventure. They recently made their home on an Indian reservation along the Columbia River. God only knows what they are up to now.

> Integrity works best in a context of love and respect.

I am convinced that integrity is the very nectar of life and it works best in a context of love and respect. For example, during World War II many God-fearing, moral people, chose to systematically and strategically lie to hide Jewish people from the Nazis. They had made the choice within their value system that lying to protect life was a more noble choice than telling the truth to the Nazis. They showed great integrity. I'm sure you or I would have made the same choice.

> Those who live lives of understanding and compassion are the real heroes of our time.

We need to put integrity at the top of our value system, honor it in all occasions, vote for people who demonstrate it in their lives, practice it in our schools and career pursuits. We must put integrity above our personal differences—we must be honest with others, even if they have views different from our own. We must put integrity above our appetite for money and power and be honest even though it may get in the way of our career goals.

We must place integrity at the cornerstone of our personal growth. Those who live a life of understanding and compassion are the real heroes of our time. We must make *them* the trend setters, the crusaders, and the real ministers, politicians, and leaders.

How Fluid are Truth and Integrity?

I remember a debate on truth at a recent education seminar. The statement was made that there was no truth and that we could never know all things, so, how could we really claim anything as real truth? In addition, it was proposed that reality is only what we make it to be. After searching my heart, I said, "Perhaps I'm stupid, but this statement makes no sense to me."

Remember, Pilate also asked, "What is truth?"

If there were no concepts of truth to build on in science, architecture and music, how would anything go together? Go together based on what? How can any therapist say there is no truth if we really believe suicide is wrong? How can we really believe in anything if we don't believe the *constant* that life is precious?

God is the basis for all our values and integrity.

The bottom line is this: If a loving God being hadn't lovingly creating us, we wouldn't be here. Nor would we have a basis for establishing values and integrity. Where would we draw power and truth from? Who is qualified to give the standard?

When operating in a mindset of integrity, we become empowered by our own choices. Others will respect and honor us more than we can ever know because we stand for truth and honor.

Others will respect and honor us more than we can ever know if we stand for truth and honor.

I want to share with you my own most cherished values and beliefs. They include the following:

God is God and I am human.

I want to know God, so I will try by loving others and communicating with God my appreciation for the gift of life.

More than anything I want people to know how precious and uniquely powerful they are.

Dr. Roth privately wondered if her topic 'Integrity in Hollywood' was popular.

Regardless of differences in other's experience I will honor and love others by respecting differences in faith and opinion.

Differences will not hurt me. I have a primary directive that values loving God, others and myself.

I believe in an environment of truth and love in which individuals can work out their unique and intimate journey. It is crucial to respect differences in timing, perception, experiences and stages of personal acceptance.

I am not where you are, and you are not where I am, but we can reach into each other's heart and space with love.

I will not quit. Trying is the only vehicle I can succeed in.

I will practice understanding, forgiveness and compassion.

I will lovingly continue to challenge the fabric of my developing integrity, asking myself always how honest I am being with myself, others and God?

I will practice the mindset of success and expect positive things even in life's trials.

I will practice forgiving myself when I screw up. I will also practice forgiving others.

Soul food—feeding the hungry inner self

You have to feed your core identity. It roars like a hungry lion and must have food to live. Depending on the choices you made somewhere along the line to give up or empower yourself, your inner self will cry out hungrily for certain kinds of food. If deep down inside you have a blueprint for worthlessness and failure, your inner self will either hunger for the dark, temporary power of deceit, unforgiveness, lack of understanding, pride and dishonesty. If instead you have a blueprint for empowerment, your inner self will hunger for those foods that develop it—hard work, carefully reasoned decision making, self-honesty and so on.

Switching from junk food to soul food is not easy, but it's easier than you think because you have a great Helper. As I started to fill my body with life-giving foods, I realized God had cared for me on every level that ministered to my inner self. I gave God my pride and embarrassment. God taught me appreciation. I gave God my arrogance and need to control life's circumstances. God gave me true self esteem, purpose and the power of humility. I gave God my good taste and desire for fame and fortune. God showed me wealth in a flower and a sunset.

Use God's guidance and feed your inner self the food it really needs.

Soul food (stock your kitchen well)

Clean out the lies and distortions about your worth.

Meditate on truth daily.

Make clear decisions based on reason.

Treat people with respect.

Being one with God constitutes a powerful majority. Don't let another lost person rob your power, hopes and dreams. Rise up and be heard.

Being one with God constitutes a powerful majority.

Imagine what you want to be like, and practice your vision from the viewpoint of your future reality, and then watch yourself become all you ever wanted.

Establish what you can be thankful for. There is power in the act of thankfulness. Learn to appreciate small and large things and learn to be thankful for just life itself, you can withstand almost anything. First, stand.

When you realize that God is, and you are, everything else in life is an adventurous bonus.

Create a positive environment from which to grow. Do not wait for someone to come rescue you to a better environment. Take steps today to clean up your own.

Misery loves company. If all your friends are negative and drain you, it's time to reassess your balance: Would it be better for you to seek out supportive, **positive new friends**, or should you discuss your concerns and commitments in order to grow with your current friends? Be honest; if your old friends can't adopt, then, painful as it may seem, you must leave them.

Your inner self needs positive, healthy food to have any positive impact on yourself and others, so search yourself and write down areas and situations that drain your energy and peace of mind. Face them and deal with them. You are in control, not the energy drainers.
Develop and practice the mindset of success—look for the good, even in pain and suffering.

Learn the power of focus

In Tai Kwon Do I learned that anyone can do their forms, but forms have no affect or beauty without focus on each move, combined with intensity. **I'm convinced one of the key reasons people stay stuck, or continue to give up, is that they have never really learned to harness their innate energy and focus in an impactful way.** A kick can break tissue or break four boards depending on your will and focus. So learn to focus on what you really want. Too many people get discouraged when their efforts at personal achievement aren't immediately rewarded. It wasn't that they weren't talented, worthy, or skilled enough—they just weren't focused.

In order to focus on the successful completion of your goals and dreams, you must first harness power by feeding the inner self. You can't focus what you don't have. As I've said before, if you don't feed those inner-self attitudes and behaviors that keep your inner strength from

draining out, you will have a difficult focusing on positive new attitudes. Discouragement will continue to reinforce the primary directive of failure.

Martial arts was a great practice arena for stretching my limits and teaching me to harness power and focus. Others find other disciplines that are just as effective. But whatever discipline you choose, set your goals and then focus positively.

Focus on giving yourself permission to be excellent, listen honestly and see clearly.

Developing the ability to focus really involves giving yourself permission to see all that wants to be seen on different dimensions of your life. Focusing is the art and practice of really listening to the content and intent of a communication or working out the details of a health and fitness program. For example, focus on following through with a daily nutritional plan. What is it going to cost? What types of exercise will it take? What muscle groups need attention? What are the physical objectives? How will you reward yourself along the way, instead of sabotaging the little steps of success with a binge. How can you set yourself up for success along the way? Is there a friend who can work with you?

Remember, lack of focus is really a symptom of not giving yourself permission to be excellent, listen honestly and see clearly. Focus implies honesty, courage, power and direction. First get honest with yourself, then focus, then conquer.

Learn to Rest, Relax and Play

Some of us are going nowhere, but really fast.

In this society, we have hung the "shoulds" and "expectations" of our work and ambition on the wrong primary directive. This directive pressures us to work and perform without ceasing in every area of our lives except our inner selves. For many this ethic continues to dominate right into the bedroom. Our houses become our prisons.

For the compulsive worker a house is often a prison.

If we ran cars and planes the way we run our stress-filled lives, most of us would be dead inside a year from all the massive wrecks and breakdowns. Do we have to look at car engines to understand our essential need for maintenance and rest? Medical data clearly reflect that stress is a major cause of disease. We are a extremely stressed people, a sure sign of internal confusion and unhappiness. We must learn to relax and rest.

Be creative at rest. At work, just close your eyes for one minute and let your muscles go limp. Meditate or just let your mind wander for one or two minutes. Then open your eyes. Take a deep breath, stretch and get back to your busy world.

In Tae Kwon Do, sometimes my heart rate would get too high in our workouts, so I learned to take even a 30 second break and relax my body by closing my eyes, letting my muscles go limp while breathing deeply. It was amazing how this little exercise replenished my energy reserve enough to get through the practice.

Walking briskly is an excellent activity that is great for relaxation and exercise, because it is safe and gets your heart rate up and blood flowing. I walk three or four miles a day with my dogs. I have more energy now to do more in my day, and I have seen my muscles tone up.

Other ways to relax include the following: Take a bubble bath; bake cookies; read a good book; go to coffee with a friend; write a letter; listen to music; make a fire and stare into it; go swimming; hike; camp; take a drive in the country; get a massage; write down your dreams and goals; pray; let yourself be held; experience a head or foot rub (they are wonderful). Make up your own relaxation list and start relaxing, you are worth it.

Exercise, breathe, eat right, and drink lots of water.

Part of the empowerment process is to realize the relationship between body, mind and spirit. **A house doesn't serve us very well with just a roof or just a foundation**. We need to build the walls, fit them to the foundation and match them to the wires and pipes and relate them to the decor…. It doesn't do a whole lot of good to accept yourself and feel good inside, only to let your body rehearse old, self-destructive behaviors. Without enough movement to get your heart going, your body is really functioning in slow motion.

The first steps are the hardest. But you will start to feel self-respect immediately as you try. You notice this even before you notice physical improvements. Even though those first steps are hard and physical rewards seem so far away, focus on the act of courage you are demonstrating by starting. Feel the empowerment and energy in your own courage to make a positive choice. Your future reality has already happened in the first steps you take. Your fit and toned body is already inside you.

There are all kinds of fun ways to move and get your blood flowing. You can walk, jog, ride a bike or jump rope. You can develop muscle tone by flexing different muscles even while sitting at work, on a plane or at home. When standing in line try putting more weight on one leg than the other. Then reverse the process. Muscle pressure and resistance is a great way to tone those muscles.

Exercise does not have to cost money. I do curls and push-ups at home or on the road. It's also fun to dance around (just move your body) to music. Make moving fun. You are literally breathing life into yourself by moving, and *you do have time for it if you think* you *are worth maintaining.*

You are literally breathing life into yourself by moving.

While in heavy training for my black belt, I drank a lot of purified water. You can't imagine how good it feels to purge your system naturally. I recommend drinking lots of water. It will assist in the flush-

That cow tried to sneak in last week's Focus Walk!

ing and detoxifying process. Before I really started exercising and drinking water, I would get a lot more intestinal cramps and feel constipated. We are not designed to stay still and not flush out old food and toxins. Keep yourself as fresh as possible. It will make a huge difference in your attitude in general. Drink lots of water.

Drink lots of water to help detoxify and purify yourself.

I have also learned to eat a minimum of red meat and a lot more fish, turkey and chicken. My trainers always encouraged me to eat fresh food. I feel much more energy now that I eat more vegetables, fruit and grains. I found optimum energy and little or no fat in black beans, brown rice and vegetables. These are also inexpensive foods that can be adorned with spices. Remember, your system is far more deserving of attention and service than your car.

Remember, your system is far more deserving of attention and service than your car.

Don't Forget to Play

Part of your essential refueling process is play. Let those inhibitions of pain and "learned adulthood" come down. Take small risks and let your joyful, curious side come out. It is okay to laugh too loud, make funny, spontaneous sounds and cry at strange times. As you make choices to start living and loving yourself, you must begin to recognize that an essential part of empowerment is play.

Just start in and develop your playground. My playground looks like this: I play by telling jokes and goofing off with my friends. I play in Tae Kwon Do. I walk my dogs and wrestle with them. I sing, play the piano and fantasize about my dream ranch with horses. I plan my dream vacation, make huge, weird looking cookies, go to action and science fiction movies, go target shooting, dabble in network marketing and am always looking for new adventures.

Develop loving relationships (We really do need each other)

The whole concept of being vulnerable to others has been the

Suddenly, in a session of scream therapy, Dr. Roth wondered if she was too old to change her career.

biggest paradox in my life. Over the years in my secret heart of hearts I've craved intimacy and love, and yet I have often acted tough, edited my reactions and been too haughty on the surface. I recall, in response to my endless childhood accidents, feeling embarrassed at attention and pushing away emotional comfort. Part of my strongest beliefs were tied up with the myth that I had to act strong and not risk deep emotion with others. I remember even pushing my parents away from any expression of my true feelings when I felt vulnerable. I let my love for them be shown with gifts and controlled emotion. I began to develop a private inner world of fantasy and intimacy. I learned in my mind that I didn't have to risk, didn't have to be rejected and thereby could control. I created a mythological kingdom where I ruled. Part of its power came from the pride of tricking others and my real self into submission.

The distance between my *presented* self and *inner* self became wider as I chose to receive love only in my secret world of my imagination. Even though I had always being a care giver, genuinely carrying and empathizing with other people's pain, I hadn't convinced myself I was worthy of love, because I felt ugly, overweight and unpopular. I would only give it and not allow myself to receive it.

I wrote the following song when I was 18 in response to my emerging desire to be fully genuine with others. Many have the feeling that they give out, but have trouble getting in. It was a critical transition time on my journey of risk taking.

"I'm a doll"   by Laurie Roth

[Sometimes if we just sit and listen to one another,
real intimacy would find it's way to us.]

I'm a doll, upon a shelf.
I sit here and look pretty,
Singing lullabies to myself.
Tell me why are you sitting here with me?

In this dark corner of the room it's hard to see—
Would you like a cup of tea?
I hate to leave. It's been such fun,
But you're too close, it's time to run.
And, why the light, it burns my eyes,
Turn on the dark,don't see me cry.
And yes it hurts, the way you glow,
My shell's too thick,I cannot grow.
Please don't push, don't make me fall,
I have no legs, I only crawl.
But, would you teach me to stand?
Or would you please take my hand?
And would you learn my name,
and please remember my pain, my friend.

Loving is like anything else that is empowering. It depends on your ability to take charge of your own destiny and giving yourself permission to experience it. It flows through you as you take little steps and it builds confidence and self-respect. Love is the balm of healing. It is your rightful inheritance as a precious human being and awaits your command. Remember you are worth it, so practice giving and receiving love.

Finally, as you jump into your new "risking" arena, realize this. Just as you learn how to drive a car, perform a new job and learn how to cook, you also need to give yourself time to learn how relationships heal and grow. Here are a few guidelines for opening out to others and yourself:

1. Get to know yourself; write down your desires, wants and needs you dared not mention before.

2. Practice sharing these with a friend or loved one.

The Russian triplets insisted Dr. Roth first demonstrate limbo therapy.

3. Practice role playing with a loved one. How might you both tackle a problem and at the same time show respect and support to each other?

4. Put on your success mindset and seek understanding in all areas of your life. Also offer understanding to others.

5. Practice actively listening to your friend or loved one and then paraphrase what you thought you heard.

6. Compliment your friends and loved ones, and remind each them daily of your love.

7. Introduce surprises and spontaneity into your relationships; fantasize, dream and explore these new realms with those close to you.

8. Romance is as romance does. Start in with soft words, rubs, touches, hand holding, walks on the beach, sensual looks, candles, escape weekends, passionate love making, holding, hot tubs, dinners out. Make lists of new things to try—then try them. You create the spark—it doesn't magically fly into your life. You create room for it.

9. Build a business, try a project, or join a club with someone you care for deeply. Create new fun and growth-oriented experiences.

10. Take charge of your journey. Plan with a loved one how you are going to achieve your goals and dreams. How, when, where, with who? How will you continue to fuel your energy and love?

Waking Up Exercises (Some tips on how to move toward empowerment):

1. If you want more time to relax and lay back, first look at what is behind the endless activity treadmill you are on. Ask yourself these

question: Whose drum are you marching to? And why? Are you hiding from yourself in endless activity? Are you afraid of the success you might feel if you actually focused on yourself and achieving your own goals? Once you have determined that you are worth maintaining and supporting, inform those in your inner circle. Then activate your plan. Focus and get specific about how you want to relax and play, when and how often. What activities are free? Which, cost money? Survey your daily and weekly schedule. Write down your needs as a key factor of everyday.

2. Try increasing your the sharpness of your focus-level in your relationships. Practice listening to your loved ones instead of tuning out or interrupting, while anticipating their next response. Don't invite people into your house only to space out at the TV. Learn to focus on the moment of communication. What words are being said? What gestures and tones do you notice? How do you feel? Focus on giving an honest, respectful and clear response that owns your feelings. Practice listening to each other for fun. Make it an activity in which you and a significant other pick a subject of interest or shared challenge and talk to each other about it. Make growth fun, not irritating.

3. With a partner, take turns actively focusing and listening to one another. Paraphrase or reflect what you thought you heard from your partner as a respectful perception check. The best communication assumes little. It checks in respectfully, reflects empathy, questions gently and paraphrases so the listener makes sure he or she understands the intent of what was being shared. This is all involved in the art of focus. As you gain more internal confidence and give yourself permission to succeed, you will notice your enhanced ability to focus and follow through with more sensitive listening skills—with exercise, dieting, prayer, rest, play, romance, sexuality, work and all kinds of small and large adventures and goals.

Dr. Bachneeny demonstrates the new "Brief Therapy" for type A clients.

CHAPTER 16:

SETTLING IN

*"So what if a window broke—take advantage of the fresh air
while you wait for the new one."*

Successfully Reaching Your Goals

Once you start to fill up with a sense of worth and begin choosing attitudes and behaviors that bring you energy and self respect, it's time to take charge. It's time to set goals. The self-help industry is full of goal-setting programs and propaganda. I remember the other day I heard a typical business opportunity advertisement on the radio that said, "For those of you who can focus and set goals call us at..." For some time I have been troubled with the goal- setting rhetoric which so often assumes that all you have to do is set a goal and that's all there is to it. Supposedly desire alone can suddenly fulfill those goals and bring you success.

Desire alone is never enough to attain a goal.

I have never seen desire alone build anything, much less a house.

My own experiences with setting goals and struggling with the follow-through process taught me there was more to achieving goals than just wanting to achieve them. How many times in our lives have we set worthwhile, professional or personal goals and started out with great intentions, only to watch our energy and interest scatter soon after we began?

Let's look at the process that follows after you set a goal. **When you first set a goal you are operating from a fresh vision and sense of purpose**. This energizes you. It heralds the beginning of your race to achieve your goal. You may have set a goal to lose weight, start a workout program, pursue a business opportunity or spend more time alone with your family. Whatever your goal was, you were primed and could imagine the finish line.

Then, with the race started and energy flowing, you move forward on the course. At this point, usually about a third of the way into the course, the initial burst of energy and sparkle has been replaced with hard work. You begin to notice a drop in your energy level and begin to experience the temptation to go back to familiar ground. Another voice starts to tempt you to reward your first bold efforts by bringing on a meal or skipping your workout schedule or forgetting about time for yourself because you're too busy again.

At this point if you don't understand that such feelings and temptations to quit or relapse are normal, you will feel like a failure. Your energy and desire to continue will wane, and you will have yet another excuse to slip into the familiar "failure mindset."

As you start pursuing your goals, you are stretching stale muscles and at the same time learning how to live in a "success mindset". This feels new and can be frightening in its unfamiliarity. So your creative and intelligent mind tries to throw up seductive allurements to get you back to its former comfort zone. That comfort zone depends on failure and counts on lack of follow through for its survival. If deep down inside you believe you are worthless, no matter what spurts of courage you drag up to start a project, you will probably fail because you haven't changed your negative blueprints.

> If deep down you believe you are worthless, no matter how hard you try you will probably fail.

When you first start working on your goal, you should expect challenges to confront you. Don't be surprised by the hurdles—it's the nature of any race toward success. When you are new to feelings of self worth and unfamiliar with how to succeed, you can become quickly discouraged at the first sign of a challenge. To complete your goals, you must learn to draw from motivational assets other than just "good feelings." I discuss some of those on the following pages.

Speaking of challenges....my grandparents got married the year the great depression was at its worst. They were dirt poor, but were lucky enough to have been given an old car. After their wedding they took off on their "honeymoon," which meant they were going to stay with their in-laws. On the way there all four tires flattened. Grandpa drove the last 20 miles on wheels alone. A month later they decided they needed their own place to live but had no money and grandpa could only get odd jobs. So rather than give up he tore down an old barn, unbent the nails, used the old wood and built their first house. Sometimes it's not the goal that is the problem, but our ability to see the possibilities.

SOME WARMING UP ACTIVITIES

1.Ground Rules for Setting Successful Goals.

The first and most important ground rule is that you are not *trying* to be successful. You already are. Why? Because you exist and God has already established your worth. Your real goal is to accept your life as an adventure, an experiment in the laboratory of living. When you do that, you begin to believe in your capabilities and are setting goals that stretch your limits to encompass those of your huge house. Your goal becomes the ever-expanding commitment to exploring the joys of living.

Just as a race car driver has check points and pit stops, you need to approach your goal program the same way. Expect before you even start that along the way you may meet obstacles, get bored with the details or get discouraged with the hard work. But keep viewing each turn and bump in the road as part of your adventure. Resist quitting.

2. Have a Clear Picture of Your Completed Goal.

Fear often has to do with the unknown. Our imagination and creativity can enhance our ability to stay on our goal achievement course or it can work against us. Rehearsing negative fears and *what-ifs* can sabotage our course. When setting a goal from your Dreams and Wishes Catalog, you must demystify it. Make it crystal clear. If your goal is to lose 30 pounds, then you start on your journey by visualizing how you already look in your very near future. Cut out pictures of healthy people that resemble your desired look. Tape them up everywhere—in the bathroom, bedroom, at work, in your car, wallet and kitchen. Put that picture all around your goal track.

We often fear what we don't know. So what's the solution to fear?

Next, interview a fit person and ask questions about how he or she managed to get fit and *stay* fit. Ask questions about their journey:

"How did you lose or gain weight?"

"What do you eat?"

"How do you continue to be motivated and keep weight off?"

"How long did it take to achieve your goal?"

"How did you encourage and reward yourself along the way?"

Don't just picture part of your completed goal, but picture yourself in the context of your completed goal. Picture this: You are now fit and look fabulous. Picture walking confidently down a beach with others admiring you. Picture traveling, boldly meeting new people with your improved confidence. Imagine catching the eye of someone admiring you. Fantasize the new you in your new world, in your new mansion.

The Bean family can now jump again after realizing just how important beans are.

3. Write down the details of your goals.

For example, you want to lose 50 pounds in four months, starting in June so you can be in your new body by September. The low fat food program I will use is…. It will cost…. My food rewards will be….

4. Identify Current Feelings And Situations.

Now, write down the feeling details of your goal.

a. How do I feel now about myself at my current weight?

b. *At work*: What comments or situations cause me to feel bad, insecure, afraid or depressed? List feelings and situations at work.

c. *At home:* What comments or situations from significant others hurt me? List feelings and situations. Establish a baseline of your feelings.

d. *With friends/society:* What comments or situations cause me to feel bad? List feelings linked to specific comments and situations.

5. Study your Empowered feelings.

Write down the feeling details of your completed goal:

a. *At work:* Put yourself back in those painful business and work situations, see yourself acting confident, taking risks, being charming, funny and forgiving. Think positive thoughts about the insensitive people in your life. Your real power is in your ability to forgive, be gracious and grow in your own power. Don't give rage away; give only love. Keep the center of your power.

b. *At home:* Put yourself back in those situations with your significant others. What do they say now? How do they act to your new and improved self? How do you feel about the

Richey, if you breathe on me again, you will be sensing an empathetic sidekick upon your left temple.

change in attitude towards you? Inform them of any hurt feelings you experience. Maybe you now feel accepted only because you are fit. Write down and describe the good feelings about your new attention and praise, but also acknowledge possible painful adjustments and discussions you may need to have as you appear more empowered and fit. Fear often has to do with the unknown. Make everything about your goal known.

Fear has to do with the unknown. What is the best remedy for fear?

c. *With friends/society:* Put yourself back into societal situations with your new look. How do people behave now? How do you react to you? Don't let negative people affect you. People are often cruel because of a strong lack of self-love and the healthy ability to put things in true focus. Seek understanding as you visualize your new self relating to new responses from society and friends.

d. As you prepare to enter your course, visualize your goal. Write it. Feel it. Now work with what has already happened into your present reality.

6. Understand the course before you enter the track.

To avoid setting yourself up for failure, you must know the course. How long is it? Who has also done it before and what was their experience? What are the expected financial, emotional and physical challenges that exist on the course? What sort of hurdles could be thrown in your way? What is your strategy to get over them? Following is a brief story that I think illustrates the above points:

When I rejoined Tae Kwon Do in November, 1994, I was out of shape, having been away from competition since 1990. I knew if I had any real desire to get my black belt I had to give myself permission to succeed and to learn about the steps and

After a day of listening to tramatic stories Dr. Roth imagines a world with no coffee.

obstacles on the course.

The first challenge I had to face was entering an open martial arts tournament that same month. Part of the requirement for a black belt was to compete at one or two tournaments before May 20, which was the black belt finish line.

In addition to competing at tournaments, I had to achieve 475 points out of 500 in a pentathlon on May 6, 1995. If I passed my events in long distance running, speed swimming, weight lifting, pull ups, sit ups and push-ups, I could try for my black belt on May 20th. Here I would have to break three boards with any kick and a hand strike, competitively spar another brown or black belt, do two forms and some three-step fighting routines.

When I started my course at the first tournament, I was in poor shape. I was insecure, poverty stricken, depressed and basically stressed out. I remember the day of the event, looking around at the familiar sea of martial arts contestants, only now they were faster, younger, and operating with an edge of confidence I didn't have. I recall trying to visit with some of the brown and black belt women. I was attempting to break the ice and make myself relax, but it appeared that most of the women were aloof and operating in their killer instinct mode.

As our section of the tournament started, I couldn't help noticing the lethal looking line up in which I would be fighting. This one red belt was particularly ferocious looking. She had two coaches hovering over her, chanting something. I was sure it was "Kill Laurie, Kill Laurie, Kill Laurie." It's funny how when you have made a decision to pursue a goal, insecurity and terror think they are invited along.

Much to my horror, the judges paired me with her. My life flashed before my eyes. I saw my second grade year fly by, then third, fourth, (fifth was a bad year so I quickly moved on to) sixth, seventh, and eighth. Soon we were called to the ring—me, the unfit, 34-year-old failure who couldn't remember any of her previously learned forms, and her, the young 22-year-old nuclear missile from hell. Why did my first obstacle on my goal course have to be her? Couldn't it just as easily have been a 4' 2", ninety pound woman recovering from a car accident? But no. I had to take on the forces of hell, my first day on the track. Okay...enough whining. I was in the ring now. I had to bow, raise my head and fight.

When the judge announced the beginning, I vaguely remember, in my pre-coma state, receiving several punches to the chest, head, and arms. It only took seconds for my impressive form to land quite unimpressively on my behind. I got up, and the flurry of attacks continued, with me barely able to defend myself. I got knocked on my behind a second time. It was the second time I was thrown down that a news flash entered my head: "Alert. Red Alert—you believe you are losing so you *are* losing. You haven't tried to score because you are letting her power smother and intimidate you. Where are your assets?"

Also, while on my behind the second time, I realized I had a secret weapon (although out of practice and rusty). She didn't know about my flexible, face high round house kicks. I used to win tournaments in the 80's with my kicks alone, but right then I had to decide if I was a failure, unfit to succeed, or if I was worth trying my best. When I got up, I had decided I would try my kicks. Even if I lost I would try my best to face this scary creature. As I got up and the flag dropped, I went crazy. All the pain and rage of my past year went into my kicks. She threw her flurry of punches, but this time I ducked and nailed her with two roundhouse kicks and a sidekick. I scored. I remember the stunned look of horror in her eyes and the warnings yelled from her coaches, "Watch out for her face high kicks—watch the face kicks!" But it was too late, I kicked her again in the head, then faked her out with two more kicks. I scored. By the time the match ended I had won by one point.

7. Establish Steps That Fit Your Empowered Stride.

Part of setting yourself up for success involves not just clearly visualizing your goal, but taking the steps to get there. A lot of times people new at risking and goal setting focus heavily on the fantasy part, the end product. It is fun and inspiring to imagine yourself the rich business entrepreneur, the famous singer, or gorgeous babe. But to get there you must set practical, realistic, well-researched steps. When I first began to get serious about my goal to be an accomplished singer, I brainstormed on paper all the possible challenges and steps I could think of. Then I asked others their opinions—studio owners, local producers and DJs. I then consulted with an attorney about how to create fund-raising structures, what paperwork was needed and what kind of seed capital.

Doing the research and brainstorming phase is critical before you launch. Wouldn't you want a pilot to understand the plane before he flew it off the runway? Learn to be visionary and practical at the same time. It is important to understand that the two principals do go together and each facilitates the other. The glamour and hoopla at the finish line come only as the result of your practical, researched steps.

It is also essential, as you begin your course, to set your stride long enough that you feel out of your comfort zone. Stretch yourself a little bit. When you are setting new goals and operating from a success mindset, you are likely to take smaller steps than you are really capable

Reframe your scary feelings about challenges as essential, necessary steps toward growth and empower-ment.

of, because of your memory of old comfort zones. As a new and improved goal setter, you anticipate those times when you feel compelled to run back to negative "I can't" thinking. **Listen to yourself and ask yourself how many times you say to yourself or another, "I can't do this."** "I've never done this, or, it's not my style." "I'm not that way, I'm a failure."

Our culture is plagued with negative conditioning that invites us to stay stuck in small steps that go in a circle leading no where. Learn to re-frame those awkward, scary feelings as essential and wonderful. They are only reflecting your steps of courage, growth and empowerment. Comfort only comes with practiced repetition, understanding your course and following through on it.

8. What Type Of Energy Does Your Goal Need To Succeed?

Many people establish their goal while underestimating the relationship between mind, body and spirit. How much mental and emotional emphasis do you think it took for me to get a black belt? Far more than physical. The physical outcome was only an extension of the mental empowerment I had created. The strike and power came from my rehearsed desire, mental practice and discipline.

If your goal seems like an emotional one, chances are it involves heavy mental and physical fuel to for you to reach that finish line. For instance, you may want more intimacy in your marriage. Learning to receive and give intimacy involves risk and positive mental rehearsal about you and your partner's worth. I have had many clients over the years who have desired intimacy but were not reinforcing this desired goal with positive mental practice. They were still making negative statements to themselves, denying the permission to feel love. They then wondered why desire for their physical goal was not enough.

If your goal is a physical, or weight goal, realize that without planning to support yourself with your mental and physical resources you are in trouble. Part of my goal achievement portfolio is attending to and drawing energy from my spirit. I remind myself of God's love for me and others. This rehearsal and meditation affirms the healthy big picture and context of my goals. It feeds the power of love which cultivates courage to be.

To fulfill any worthwhile goal you must build your support and energy plan.

What positive thoughts are you going to focus on that remind you of your worth and your ability to achieve? What ways are you gaining emotional support for yourself and your goal? Have you set up an accountability and encouragement structure with others?

Finally, you need to move your body, get adequate rest and get your blood flowing. Just the release of pleasure chemicals from exercise makes you feel more positive. You are a whole person—draw from whole assets.

9. Reward Yourself Along The Way.

"Come on let's have a cup of coffee before we put up another wall."

One of the things I would look forward to and sometimes focus on while running was having coffee after the run. It was a reward and special time of sharing I could look forward to. Every Saturday after Tae Kwon Do practice I would go out to coffee with my buddies; and on Sunday mornings, with my running partners. This routine really made the whole process of the hard physical work enjoyable, because I had rewards built in. Often, just the anticipation of this little reward would help me through the hard spots.

As I began to get fit, I went dancing more often, which also was

Often the anticipation of a reward is enough to keep you pursuing you goal.

exercise, only much more fun to me. This activity also represented a personal reward and place of expression. I also began to take little risks showing off my better figure. I wore swimming suits, shorts and mini skirts. I was growing in my confidence, working hard and rewarding myself along the way.

Put your accountability and encouragement team together. Remember that there are often down times along the path of fulfilling worthwhile goals. These are times when your will power is weak and when you're ready to give up. At these times you need to remind yourself visually and in writing what your goal looks like and evaluate the challenge directly in front of you. Also, draw from the assets you have, such as your partners, friends and associates. When you've made yourself accountable to someone it's harder to give up. These people can also act as coaches and encouragers when you are feeling threatened or maxed out. It's much better to ask for a little encouragement and assurance than to quit and go back to the starting line defeated.

It is in the nature of change to take risks and stretch your limits. Assume at the starting line that sabotage attempts will hit you like bombs dropping in a video game. Be ready in advance with your asset tool kit and conquer all of your intruders. You may find that most of the obstacles you face come from within. Resist the temptation to retreat to your safe and negative comfort zone.

Listen to your own negative self-talk and write down how many times you cancel out yourself by blaming, avoiding, whining and making endless excuses why you can't do something. Realize that all these negative habits do is support your giving up and failure structure.

Finally there comes a time of choice: you can choose to continue to rob yourself or snap out of it and start acting like the worthwhile person you are. God can't make you choose life. Therapists can't make you healthy. Your spouse, mom or dad can't make you whole. Nothing outside you can make you do it. You make you do it. Now get started!

10. Set Short And Long Term Goals—Enter A Life-style Of Growth.

Establishing goals is much more than obsessive, hard work and activity. It is a reflection on your power set in healthy motion. This empowered identity defines life in terms of its many adventures, not in terms of its many obstacles and failures.

Setting your goals typifies the acceptance of your worth and the value in resources you have. These resources are obtained from suffering and loss, as well as from joys. It's all about heightening your awareness and desire for life and entering its celebration.

As you begin to understand who you really are, the desire to taste and soak up experiences draws you on a path of growth. You get off the sidelines. You may have looked at the same mundane landscape with the same boring characters for years. But as you come to accept yourself and take responsibility for your growth, you may be astonished at the wonderful new colors and shapes of things.

You may find yourself saying, "My, how my friends and surroundings have changed." In reality when we begin to feel hope within ourselves and no longer live like out-of-control victims, we can't help seeing people, events and surroundings in a more positive light. When we begin to operate from a combination of love and wisdom, our outlook on almost everything changes.

Learn to respect yourself because you survived loss and failure and took the assets from your losses. Notice how fear of the unknown starts to dissipate as you begin to explore new possibilities in life. Embrace them as they come. You can't fail—you can only experience living. Here's a brief success story from out of my family's history:

She was poor and had spent most of her childhood caring for her 11 brothers and sisters on a farm. As an adult she cared for her invalid husband. She never had the "glory" jobs. Instead she worked at a small cleaners in The Dalles, Oregon. Though she felt very ordinary, she had always had a dream of being a nurse, even as a young girl. But because of the way life played out for her she had not been able to obtain a high school diploma. But she was a determined woman and still retained that lifelong dream. So at age 58 she got her GED and entered a community college. She obtained straight As in nursing and graduated when she was 60. For ten years she had a rewarding career in nursing and then retired. That amazing woman was my Grandmother Rue.

When you begin identifying your dreams and goals, don't get stuck with just the original version. Look at the essence of what is in your dream. Focus on what it is about that dream that really has meaning for you.

Though my Grandmother Rue had always wanted to be a nurse and life seemed to have dealt her a different hand, let's take a look at how that dream survived.

As a young girl, Grandma Rue took care of her brothers and sisters—she was a nurturer, a caregiver. As a mature woman my grandmother devoted much of her life to her invalid husband; again, she was a caregiver. Who's to say the essence of her dream wasn't always really to be a caregiver, and being a nurse was only one way of realizing that?

When you set a goal that is flexible and understandable, take that flexibility and use it to solve the challenges you face trying to attain it. If lack of money is your challenge, brainstorm, research and ask endless questions until you get your portfolio of possible answers to draw from. Don't give up. Instead maybe you could scale up or down. Try a different time frame or get partners or just muscle it through.

Achieving anything that is worthwhile involves your commitment first to yourself and then to your goal. Finally, understand that if you have not taken the time to establish what is really important to you and why, you may be greeted at the finish line with emptiness and depression. Goals achieved that don't reflect your true values are unsatisfying at best.

Be honest with yourself. Learn the hows and whys of your goals. Make them adaptable, and enjoy the process.

Go and conquer!

Dudley and Earl contemplate the possibilities.

CARTOON LIST

To order additional copies of:

"In My House"

No Failure Allowed
or
Dr. Laurie's CD,

"If You Call Me"

Please write or call:

Dr. Laurie Roth Worldwide Productions
427 SW Madison, #167
Corvallis, OR 97333
Phone (541) 924-5122
Fax (541) 753-4905

For bookings, speaking engagements or concerts
please call or write:

Management: Dick St. Nicklaus
14657 SW Teal Blvd. #213
Beaverton, Oregon 97007
Phone (503) 220-6630